3

4

5

Interviewing Children and Adolescents

John Rich **Interviewing Children and Adolescents**

Macmillan

First edition 1968
Reprinted 1971, 1972, 1974

Published by
THE MACMILLAN PRESS LTD
London and Basingstoke
Associated companies in New York
Dublin Melbourne Johannesburg and Madras

SBN 333 08611 2

Printed and bound in Great Britain by
REDWOOD BURN LIMITED
Trowbridge & Esher

Contents

Introduction

Anyone working with children develops a technique appropriate to the job he is doing. The approaches are different for a teacher in the classroom, a youth-bureau detective interviewing a suspected delinquent, a psychiatrist making a diagnosis, or a youth leader meeting a new member of his club. Nevertheless all these situations do have something in common: an adult and a child are communicating with each other. This book gives an account of the factors involved in this relationship. It does not attempt to explore the special techniques used in one particular situation.

Many people (including a large proportion of interviewers who are experienced and competent in adult work) find it hard to communicate with children. I have tried to write for the newcomer to this field, and in doing so I have had to cover many points well known to the experienced worker. The first three chapters deal with interviewing in general, although giving emphasis to the problems encountered with children. The rest of the book is related more closely to child interviewing.

Most books on interviewing are written for a particular discipline, such as psychiatry or case-work, and most students learn the technique that is most appropriate to one or other of these approaches. One of the points I hope to make is that this is unfortunate, because it may lead to clumsy and inadequate interviews or even gross errors of assessment. For example,

one often sees psychiatrists in training who are quick
to spot the symptoms of emotional disorder, but who
completely misjudge the behaviour of normal children.
Not having had enough experience watching and
working with the normal, they will misinterpret
commonplace behaviour as evidence of a disorder.
One often sees teachers, when visiting their nephews
and nieces, talking to them as if they were in the
classroom. It is just as usual for the psychologist to
assume that the 'correct' approach to a child is the one
he uses in the clinic and to recommend something
similar to the harassed teacher trying to work with
forty children in a classroom, where it is completely
impracticable, even if it were appropriate for that
situation.

In trying to be practical I have had to be dogmatic.
I hope that the experienced interviewer will forgive
this, and that the inexperienced will recognise that I
am making suggestions and not giving instructions.
The interviewer's principal tool is himself and, as we
all differ from one another, we are all using different
tools. Slavish imitation of somebody else's technique is
like buying a suit or a dress because it looks nice on
somebody else. A book cannot teach you how to interview, but it may help you to learn.

One   Definition

The Shorter Oxford English Dictionary defines an
interview as 'a meeting of persons face to face,
especially for the purpose of formal conference on
some point'. A formal conference may be based on
explicit rules upon which the people concerned have
agreed; for example, the scope of the discussion may
have been decided upon, an area of common ground
that needs no further attention may be ignored, sensitive areas may be avoided, and so on. Many other
formal rules are taken for granted: it is assumed that
the participants will not use a foreign language and
will not make irrelevant personal attacks on each
other. Also their relative status is usually accepted by
both, and this determines to some extent what each
may say to the others and the tone of voice in which
they speak. It must be noted, however, that even a
formal conference is still 'a meeting of persons' and
will to some degree involve many of the personality
traits of the individuals taking part. The less formal
the interview the greater the part these traits will
play. The most common error made by untrained
interviewers is to lose sight of personal interactions –
the *informalities* – and to observe only the formalities.
A social worker interviewing a client is still a human
being talking to another human being; a teacher
interviewing a pupil is an adult talking to a child – and
also (this must never be forgotten) a human being
talking to another human being.

2 Interviewing Children and Adolescents

The man who was surprised to find that he had been talking prose all his life would no doubt be equally surprised to learn that he had been interviewing all his life. When we start 'interviewing' other people, we are not doing something completely new – we have been interviewing since we were born. In all these years, however, we have learned to make many assumptions about people, and most of us have fallen into particular habits in dealing with them. If our basic attitude to other people is defensive or patronising or seductive or distant, all our interviews will reflect this and will be effective only in those situations in which the particular attitude is the appropriate one. If we are to use interviewing as a professional technique, we must study our assumptions about people and be prepared to modify our habitual approach to them, but we must not (in fact we cannot) develop an entirely new range of behaviour.

It is often hard to persuade student case-workers and others that they know anything about interviewing at all. Before their first interviews they say desperately, 'I don't know how to begin', whereas if they met the same people at a party or in a bus they would be quite able to begin and maintain a conversation without too much strain. Meetings between two people may be placed on a continuum. At one extreme is the completely informal discussion, in the middle are more formal conferences, while the other extreme is exemplified by the old story of the psychiatrist who left his tape-recorder to listen to the new patient while he went out to coffee. Meeting this patient in the coffee-shop, he asked why she had left his office, only to be told that she had given her history so often that she had put it on tape and had left her tape-recorder talking to his tape-recorder. There is much to be said in some situations for an approach that makes no attempt to guide the discussion or to pass judgement. Unfortunately this is often so much emphasised that there is a danger of making the interview non-human altogether. For our purposes, then, an interview will be taken to include conversation anywhere on the continuum.

One of the essential qualities of an interview can be recognised by considering the difference between an orator speaking to a crowd and the same man giving his speech on the radio. The first situation is an interview of sorts, but the second is not, because there is no feed-back to the radio speech – the speaker's own behaviour is not modified in any way by the behaviour of the listeners. This point cannot be too strongly emphasised: in any interview there is always *interaction* between or among the people concerned.

If we bear in mind that an interview consists of two people talking to, and affecting, *each other*, we can see that it is merely a convenience to describe only one of them as the 'interviewer'. This title is normally given to the person of higher status or dominance in the particular situation: we say that an employer interviews an applicant or a teacher interviews a pupil. If by chance the applicant for the job was also a local judge and his prospective employer was to appear in his court, we should say that their roles were reversed and that the other man is now the 'interviewer'. It is, of course, true that the one who was dominant is now subordinate, but they are nevertheless the same people; apart from the dominant-subordinate aspect of their relationship, the other interactions of their personalities may be little changed; if they liked each other before, they will probably like each other now. If the employer had been prejudiced against the applicant because he was a Jew, he will be no less prejudiced against him in his role as a judge.

4 Interviewing Children and Adolescents

Any interview, then, has formal and informal elements. In an attempt to correct the tendency for beginners to overemphasise the formal elements, many of the examples given throughout this book will be of informal meetings between people rather than formal conferences. Further discussion requires separation of the various elements in interviews. These can be best understood by considering the hopes and intentions of the people taking part – that is, the *functions* of the interview.

Two Functions of the Interview

We can consider interviews under the following headings: fact-finding, fact-giving, manipulative, treatment, and demonstrative. However, most, if not all, interviews change their character as they progress. For this reason it is better to think of *functions* rather than *types* of interview.

Fact-finding Interviews

The main aim of these interviews, in whole or in part, is to elicit facts. The doctor taking a history, the lawyer questioning a client, the employer interviewing a candidate for a job, the social worker assessing a potential foster-parent – all are concerned primarily with fact-finding. In some of these examples the facts to be found include many of which the subject is not consciously aware, but in general both parties know what is to be communicated. It is obvious that, although the private eye may say 'Just gimme the facts, man, just gimme the facts', he has a fairly clear idea of which particular facts he wants, and the person he is questioning uses much the same frame of reference. For example, if his client said that he went from one place to another on a bus, it is not usually relevant to know the licence number of the bus or whether the conductor had a moustache. Generally speaking, the relevance or irrelevance of material is appreciated by an adult being interviewed, but the position is very different with children. The things they notice and the relative values they give to various observations are not the same as those given by the adult, and fact-finding questions have to be much more specific and direct. The danger inherent in being specific and direct is that the questions have to be based on some hypothesis, which may be confirmed without getting to the root of the problem. This point can be appreciated more easily if we place ourselves in the position of the one who is being questioned. Most of us have had the experience of accurately answering questions about a certain situation and yet failing to convey the underlying truth. This is seen most clearly in law courts, where the counsel for one side can create a totally false impression by eliciting from a witness only those facts that will help his case; it is not until the cross-examination by the other counsel that different facts, no less true and no more true, give a better perspective. It is never possible to find out *all* the facts about any situation, and an adult interviewing a child may, quite unintentionally, behave like the counsel for one side without benefit of correction by opposing counsel. This is because the roles of the adult and the child are so unequal. If the child simply answers the questions that are put to him and does not feel free enough and secure enough to explain the points that the adult did not think of asking about, the truth will never become apparent. If a child has been away from school for much of the term because of sickness and is asked 'Did you do well in your term exams?', he may answer in one of two ways: 'No', which might be strictly true, or (if he is sufficiently sophisticated and secure) 'Yes, in the circumstances'. The question was simple and direct, and although the child would have answered truthfully by saying 'No', he would not have expressed the whole truth, and the interviewer could have been misled.

This situation often presents much more of a

problem when working with children than with adults
because a child's experience is limited; and he may not
even recognise that he is being asked a question that
cannot be answered accurately without a wider range
of knowledge than he possesses.

The obsessionally careful interviewer may collect a
large number of facts that might be relevant, but
which 'over-determine' the decision. This is a common
fault with inexperienced case-workers, doctors, and
psychologists who have spent years learning how to
take 'a full history'. If the only decision to be made is
whether a child needs to be under constant supervision
(for example, if he is suicidal), there is no point in
questioning him at length on his family history or on
details of his school work. Not only is this a waste of
time, but it may cause difficulty for subsequent interviewers; most people dislike having to answer the
same questions more than once. What is more, much
unintentional communication can take place about
matters that would have been much better left alone.
For example, if the child is worried about the relationship between his parents, but has avoided thinking
about it, questions on this subject will arouse his
anxieties without dealing with them. This whole area
may need slow and careful handling at a later date, and
should be left until then. The original interview needs
to disclose just one fact – whether or not there is a
danger of suicide.

Some psychologists have an unfortunate tendency to
ask more questions than are required to solve the
intelligence, they carry out a half-baked psychiatric
problem put to them; if asked to assess the child's
intelligence, they carry out a psychiatric diagnostic
interview as well, and when the psychiatrist comes to
see the child the waters have been thoroughly
muddied. It would be equally disruptive (although it

hardly ever occurs in practice) for a psychiatrist to
allow a child to try out an intelligence test before the
psychologist examined him. I am not suggesting that
no psychologist is capable of making a psychiatric
assessment, or that no psychiatrist is capable of
administering tests – merely that each should confine
himself to the function he is supposed to perform on
each occasion.

In any fact-finding interview, except the most
superficial ones, we are dealing with truth at different
levels. For example, if a child makes it clear in an
interview that he is afraid of all adult males, it may
be a reasonable or perhaps an inescapable inference
that he has this attitude because he is afraid of his
father. But if the question is put to him – 'Is your
father kind to you?' – he may answer 'Yes' and believe
it. He may believe it because he wants to or because
he has not known what kind fathers are like. The
truth may be that Father is harsh and cruel, even
though the fact *as the child sees it* is that Father is kind.
It often happens that it is more important to know
what is 'truth' for the child than what is true in a
more general sense. In other words we have to judge
any answer by asking the following questions: is the
answer true in every sense? Is the answer false, but
does the child think it is true? Is the answer false, and
does the child know it is false? Are we dealing with
'hard' facts about which there can be no disagreement
– 'What is your name?' 'Do you like your teacher?' –
or is this a matter of opinion or value judgement? –
'Is your teacher nice?'

The essential problem facing the fact-finding
interviewer has been well expressed by Piaget:

It is so hard not to talk too much when questioning
a child, especially for a pedagogue! It is so hard not

9 Functions of the Interview

to be suggestive! And above all, it is so hard to find the middle course between systematisation due to preconceived ideas and incoherence due to the absence of any directing hypothesis! The good experimenter must, in fact, unite two often incompatible qualities; he must know how to observe, that is to say, to let the child talk freely, without ever checking or sidetracking his utterance, and at the same time he must constantly be alert for something definitive; at every moment he must have some working hypothesis, some theory, true or false, which he is seeking to check. When students begin, they either suggest to the child all they hope to find, or they suggest nothing at all, because they are not on the look-out for anything, in which case, to be sure, they will never find anything.[1]

Fact-giving interviews

The fact-giving interview is one in which the interviewer decides which facts he will give to the other person. A teacher giving a didactic lecture is carrying out such an interview. If, however, he is using a seminar type of teaching, the situation would be more correctly described as *fact-finding*, with the students playing the interviewer's role. This distinction is an extremely important one; it must be clearly understood who is deciding which facts are to be given. Forget, for a moment, the word 'interview' and remember that two people are talking. Unless one dominates the other, no problem will arise in the selection of an area for discussion because if either is dissatisfied he will insist that a different topic is pursued. If an adult is talking to a child, however, although the adult may want to receive information

[1] J. Piaget, *The Child's Conception of the World* (Harcourt, Brace, New York, 1929), p. 8.

and the child may want to give it, they can still
disagree about which information is relevant. If we
abandon our usual adult arrogance, and with it our
assumption that the adult is always the interviewer,
we can recognize that the child may be prevented from
carrying out a fact-giving interview because the adult
insists on an irrelevant fact-finding interview.

Let us suppose that a boy and his young sister have
been involved in a fight. The sister starts shouting
'Johnny hit me!' and Mother wants to know if this is
true. Johnny wants to give the facts, and as far as he is
concerned this is a 'fact-giving' interview. On the
other hand, if Mother is preoccupied with whether or
not Johnny did hit his sister, there may be a breakdown in communication because so far as Johnny is
concerned the most important point to make is that his
sister was objectionable and unfair about something –
the fact that he hit her was not of great importance.
In the course of the discussion he may give all sorts of
facts that are highly relevant to the central theme, but
Mother impatiently refuses to listen to them and
keeps asking the question, 'Did you or did you not hit
hit her?' This example illustrates an essential element
in fact-giving interviews: the person receiving the
facts has to want to receive them if the interview is
to be effective. If he does not want to, he may not
hear them at all; or if he does hear them, he will soon
forget them. This is why the seminar approach to
teaching is often much more valuable than didactic
lectures; the teacher in a seminar or discussion group
can create a question in the mind of his listener, who
then actively wants to know the answer and therefore
pays more attention when it is given. Many an adult
who says to a child in exasperation 'You just don't
listen!' is overlooking the fact that the child is not
listening because he has no particular motivation to

do so – he just isn't interested. It is amazing how
much virtually useless teaching goes on because it is
based on situations that have no appeal to the child.
Many people working with children are out of touch
with the child's world, and they miss a lot of opportunities to engage the children's full attention and
interest. It is worth noting here that 'the child's
world' is a very different thing from the world that
the adult sees around the child. If a small boy is sitting
in the classroom dreaming of being a pirate, his world
is not the classroom but the high seas.

Manipulative interviews

A frequent function of interviewing is to bring about
a predetermined change in the other person – to
manipulate him. This may be preceded by fact-finding,
but the only facts that need be elicited are those that
will enable manipulation to be effective. There is, of
course, an element of manipulation in almost any
interview because the interviewer has to bring the
other person into the frame of mind in which he will
communicate. The relationship between adults and
children is such that many of their meetings are
manipulative. If a child comes home from school
covered with mud, blood, and tears, shouting in-
coherently that Johnny rolled him in the road, the
wise mother will not carry out a fact-finding interview; she will say, 'Yes dear; your dinner's ready.
Go and wash yourself and tell me about it while you're
eating.' These two sentences are in fact a manipulative
interview, because she is concerned only with manipulating the child into a certain frame of mind. If she
had started looking for facts at this point, she would
probably have made the child even angrier or sorrier
for himself, and she would not have learned the facts
anyway. It might be noted here that the child may
allow himself to be manipulated for a number of

12 Interviewing Children and Adolescents

reasons. The advantages of his doing so may be so simple and obvious that he will readily agree; but he may be persuaded because he likes the adult concerned – in other words the adult is selling himself rather than a point of view.

The simplest (and therefore the most commonly used) method of manipulation is the use of force. This may take the form of moral blackmail – 'You will make me very unhappy if you do that' – or appear in other disguises, but force usually has the disadvantage that it loses its effect when the enforcer is no longer present.

Treatment interviews

The line between treatment and manipulation (in its broadest sense) is not easily drawn. Encouraging a disheartened child could be classified as either, but the essential difference is that manipulative interviews *impose* a change whereas treatment does not. It could be said that treatment allows the other person to develop a different attitude owing to changes in his own thinking. He may be manipulated into good behaviour, or his behaviour changes because he now feels differently.

There are many different types of treatment interviews. The simplest is the supportive one, in which the interviewer essentially listens, encourages, and sympathises as required. Another is the counselling interview, which is mainly a rational, conscious discussion of relatively clearly stated problems. The counsellor is not, of course, unaware of the client's unconscious motivations, but he does not deal with them directly. For example, a high school student may ask his school counsellor's opinion about dropping history, and point out that he is planning to take a science degree at university and that history will be of little use to him. The counsellor may happen to know

that the history teacher is like the boy's father and
that the parents separated recently. The boy may be
quite aware of this similarity, or he may be refusing
to acknowledge it, even to himself. All he knows is
that he is unhappy and disturbed in the history class
and rationalises that this is because of the subject. It is
important for the counsellor to be clear in his own
mind about whether he is carrying out a counselling
or an insight-giving interview. Some interviewers are
so delighted when they have an insight into their
client's difficulties that they simply have to share it
with him. In the circumstances mentioned above it
might do a great deal of harm to the lad if he is forced
to discuss his relationship with his father at this
particular time. The school might allow him to drop
history or it might be possible for him to transfer to a
different history class. The advice that the counsellor
gives will, ostensibly, be straightforward counselling.
Alternatively he may decide that this lad needs insight
into his underlying problem: in this case the counsellor
has to decide whether to take it up with him or
whether the boy should be referred to some other
source of help, such as a clinic.

Insight-giving interviews are considered the most
advanced and effective form of psychiatric treatment.
Insight really consists only of reformulating one's
understanding in different terms – so the insight
gained may cover a small or a large area, and may be
fairly superficial or profound. As many of the blocks
to understanding are irrational, most insight of any
real value requires something other than rational
explanation or discussion. The techniques for achieving
this belong to the realm of psychotherapy, which is
beyond the scope of this book. Other types of therapeutic interviews include reciprocal inhibition,
hypnosis, and so on.

14 Interviewing Children and Adolescents

Demonstrative interviews

This type of interview is seen when the child is 'shown off' before an audience, perhaps for clinical teaching, or on the radio or TV or in front of a group of admiring relatives. It is included here because there are dangers inherent in this situation. Children can be extremely embarrassed or resentful if information they have given to one adult, apparently in confidence, is brought out before a group of strangers. Of course, this can apply to adults too, but they are more likely to appreciate the requirements of teaching students or the need for a conference on their case; and if they give permission for a demonstration interview, they are more likely to know what they are agreeing to. Some children will agree to it without realising what they are in for and will resent appearing in front of a group; other children crave an audience and, driven either by a constitutional streak of ham or by fame-seeking parents, develop a great skill at playing 'cute'. They may succeed in pleasing an audience, but it can do them a great deal of harm by encouraging attention-seeking behaviour.

We have seen that the adult is usually in a position to force one or another type of interview upon a child, but there is still room for a vast amount of misunderstanding between them on the aim of the interview; even if the child is well aware of what the adult is trying to achieve, he may have different ideas of his own. The way in which these different aims can contradict or confuse each other is taken up in the next chapter.

Three   Co-operation, Confusion, and Conflict

Every one of us has from time to time responded to a situation with an emotion for which there is no adequate explanation. We may meet a person for the first time and take an immediate liking or disliking to him; we may be well aware of the fact that we like him, but be quite unconscious of the reason. Most people have at least one unreasonable fear, perhaps of snakes or spiders or enclosed places or heights; if this is extreme, the person's whole life may be handicapped and we call him 'neurotic'.

Just as we can move around in a familiar house – unconsciously adjusting our steps to the height of the stairs and putting a hand to a door handle without looking – all the while thinking of something completely different, so we spend our lives responding to a constantly changing social situation according to previous experience. Many of these social responses are consciously chosen, others were deliberately chosen in the past but have now become habitual. Yet others have always been irrational. If we experience any strong emotion, it may become associated with some stimulus in the environment that happens to be present at the time – for example, a tune may make us suddenly happy or sad, although we cannot remember the name of it or the situation with which it is associated.

In short, our responses to any situation are complex because we respond to all the elements that make it up.

We recognise some of these elements and know why
we respond as we do, but other elements are 'recognised' only unconsciously, and our responses to them
are unintentional.

It follows that the person being interviewed is
responding to all sorts of cues or stimuli in the
environment (which includes the interviewer). Some
of these are personal to him: the blue suit the interviewer is wearing may remind him of a loved father,
a hated uncle, a friendly postman, or a feared policeman. To some extent he will be prejudiced for or
against the interviewer because of these associations,
although he may never know, let alone say, who or
what he is reminded of. It is worth noting that the
interviewer himself may also have prejudices – in fact
from time to time he certainly will; this is unavoid-
able, and the best he can do is to recognise prejudice
when it occurs, rather than think he is making an
objective appraisal.

There are several possible sources of conflict and
disagreement in an interview. We have to recognise
contradictions between the conscious and unconscious
responses within each person, as well as contradictions
between the two people concerned. The possibilities
may be classified as follows:

1. The interviewer and subject can agree on the
purpose of the interview. This is ideal and fairly
straightforward. It may occur when a child comes
home from a party and his father asks him if he had
a good time. The father wants to know all about it
and the child wants to tell him.

2. Both can agree on the overt or official intention
of the interview, but one or other has reservations.
For example, both might agree that the function of
the interview is to reveal facts, but the subject has no
intention of giving them. Both an examiner and a

child being tested accept the same frame of reference –
that the child's knowledge is being assessed – but the
examiner wants to find out what the child really
knows, while the child wants to give the impression
of knowing a little more than he actually does.

3. They may disagree on the function of the interview, though each is aware of the other's motivation.
For example, a child is looking at toys in a store. The
salesman wants to sell and the child wants to consider,
to compare, and perhaps to select. For the salesman it
is a manipulative interview; for the child it is a fact-
finding one, though in this case each recognises what
the other is up to. The situation is reversed if a
candidate is applying for a job. Here he wants to sell
and it is the interviewer who wants to select.

4. They may disagree on the purpose of the interview, but not recognise that there is a disagreement.
This is common in work with children because often
nobody has taken the trouble to explain to the child
what the interview is all about. For example, a child
is doing badly at school and has been referred to the
psychologist from the Board of Education. The child
hears him referred to as 'Dr Jones' and knows from
experience that when you go to a 'doctor' you have a
'needle', or he may associate this interview with the
fact that he has been doing badly in class and gathers
that he is in trouble – he feels threatened. The
psychologist, on the other hand, merely wishes to take
a history and to ask questions without making any
value judgements, and he has no intention of in-
timidating the child. If the child sees the interview as
the prelude to punishment, even the most innocent
question will seem ominous: he will answer
accordingly and, if the psychologist is unaware of this,
he will be misled.

5. Either the interviewer or the child (or both) can

have a conflict within himself of conscious motivations.
If a child is in trouble and is being questioned by a
parent, the parent may want to get at the facts, but
be upset by eliciting them, and is strongly tempted to
drop the whole matter. The child may want to tell the
truth, but not want to get into trouble or upset his
mother. In this situation the conflict is not so much
between the interviewer and the child as between two
attitudes, both of them being held by each person.

6. Either the interviewer or the subject can have
an unconscious motivation that is different from his
conscious one. This is very evident in psychiatric
interviews in which the patient wants to give the
facts, but represses or 'forgets' the painful and
unpleasant ones. A highly moral businessman can
select a pretty secretary rather than a plain one and
convince himself that he has made the selection
solely on the grounds of her efficiency as a typist. The
more acutely anxious we become about recognising a
situation, the more likely we are to repress it in this
way. We may not repress it completely, but be half-
aware of our anxiety. A sixteen-year-old girl who is
preoccupied with the idea that she is physically
unattractive may begin to avoid social contacts. For
this reason she refuses office in a student society. In an
interview with a teacher who is trying to persuade her
to accept the position they may never get down to the
real cause at all, the girl bringing up all sorts of rational-
isations and excuses for refusing the job, the teacher
pointing out the advantages of taking it on. None of the
teacher's reassurances has any effect, of course, because
she is reassuring the girl about the wrong things.

7. The conscious motivations of one person can
conflict with, or tie in with the conscious motivations
of the other. This can get very complicated. For
example, a pupil and a teacher are having an argu-

ment. The child, having been brought up by an
authoritarian father feels happy in an authoritarian
situation and uneasy in an egalitarian one. His teacher
is an egalitarian and therefore prefers free discussion
with pupils to didactic imposition of opinions. The
teacher's line of argument happens to be wrong and
the child sees through it, but, because the boy is at
ease only in a subordinate role, he tries to convince
himself that the teacher is right and 'agrees' with him.
As the discussion develops the teacher recognises that
he has taken up a false line of reasoning and withdraws
from it. This makes the child very uneasy and he
becomes angry and insolent. The teacher then repri-
mands the child, not for disagreeing with him, but for
the insolence, which will of course reassure the child
because their roles are now back to 'normal'.

Teenagers, and sometimes younger children, can
be more aware of our unconscious motivations, our
prejudices and weaknesses, than we are, and can
exploit them in an interview. The pretty secretary
who was selected for the position (in the example
given above) may have been quite aware of why she
was chosen although the businessman did not
recognise it.

8. The two people concerned may mean quite
different things by the same words, and thus communicate something quite different from what they
intended. When my children were very young they
were visiting a friend of ours whose house was full of
rare and easily breakable furniture. After an hour of
rescuing antiques from infantile investigation our
friend said ironically, 'Why don't you go outside and
break some windows?' Their eyes lit up and they all
rushed out. As he relaxed, I asked 'Did you mean that
literally?' and he jumped up again saying 'Oh my
God! No!'

The way some of these conscious and unconscious motivations can shift about and be misunderstood can be illustrated in another incident between the child and the teacher described above. Let us assume that this boy has a father who rewards and punishes him inconsistently. The boy learns from this that Father is unpredictably dangerous and will generalise to all other men, seeing them as dangerous also. Let us also assume that this particular teacher is not very secure in himself. One day the boy loses his pen, and the teacher says, 'I have a spare one at home. I'll bring it for you tomorrow.' From the child's own experience at home he takes this to mean, 'I have a spare pen at home, but I'll probably forget to bring it. If I do remember, I shall keep reminding you of my generosity, and when you lose that pen I shall beat you for being ungrateful.' What the teacher really meant was, 'I took up teaching because I am a shy and lonely man and I like children. I would like you to like me.' The child actually replies, 'Don't bother, sir. Thanks all the same, I'll get one from my friend.' We know of course that he *means*, 'Look, I'd rather not get involved, because it will end up by my getting into more trouble somehow.' We can also guess that what the teacher *hears* is, 'I don't like you. None of the kids like you, and I don't want presents from you.' This is a simple, everyday, trivial occurrence. Each of them is quite wrong about the other, though each of them would genuinely like to have the other as a friend.

It must be noted that these responses might arise in any interview. If the child responds irrationally to a stimulus, he will respond irrationally to that stimulus whenever it occurs. He will do so not only if he is being interviewed by a psychiatrist looking for neurotic symptoms, but will show similar responses

when interviewed by a teacher or a prospective
employer. In other words it is as important for a
teacher to recognise neurotic responses as it is for a
psychiatrist – not so that he can carry out a treatment
interview, but so that he can avoid misinterpretation.

It is beyond the scope of this book to discuss neurotic
symptoms and behaviour. I am only pointing out that
the more a teacher knows of these matters the better
teacher he will be. Similarly, the more a psychiatrist
knows about teaching and the problems of law
enforcement and the more a police officer with a
Youth Authority knows of psychiatry and teaching
problems, the better each will be at his own work. In
short, it must never be forgotten that a child is a child
and not merely a pupil, a patient, or a delinquent.
We cannot understand him in any one capacity if we
cannot see him in the others.

All these levels of interaction take place in any
interview, but not all of them will be relevant. If a
teacher is disliked by a child, she might still have a
successful 'fact-giving' interview with him in the
ordinary course of teaching, but she might not be able
to handle him in disciplinary matters (which would
fall into our definition of 'manipulative'). On the
other hand a police officer or judge who is upset by
sex might be successful in manipulating a juvenile
sex-offender, but be unable to carry out a successful
fact-finding interview.

Even if the conscious, semi-conscious, and unconscious motivations are the same for both interviewer and child, there is the possibility of conflict if
they are not in step; that is to say, timing is very
important in the interview. A probation officer might
want to be friendly with a child, the child also wants
to be friendly with the probation officer, but the adult's
first approaches will be doomed to failure if he pushes

too hard too soon, or if he makes a gesture when the rest of the gang is around. Instead of splitting off a potentially good citizen from undesirable companions, he will only bind him more closely to them. Another adult might say, 'Don't talk to me today, I'm in a bad mood', but a child is seldom in a position to say this to an adult. The skilled interviewer will select the moment for each move with care. He probably has a number of objectives, and will decide from moment to moment which is the right one to attempt.

We have seen that the assumptions and motivations on each side are complex and operate on different levels simultaneously; that they may support or conflict with each other either within one person or between two people. This interplay keeps changing throughout the interview.

When one is trying to assess the 'success' of an interview, one has to recognise that the objectives of the two participants might have been different and contradictory. An interview could be highly successful from the child's point of view (if he is being secretive, for example), but a failure from the interviewer's (if he is trying to find out facts). Both of them might fail in what they set out to do, but succeed in other unexpected ways. It is therefore necessary for the interviewer to be able to change his objectives throughout the interview as the situation changes.

An interview need not be kept rigidly to any particular type. It is important that the overall objective be clearly understood by the interviewer beforehand; if he changes his objectives during the interview, he should know precisely why he is doing so. An example might make this clear. A child is interviewed in a clinic because he is behaving badly in school and in the neighbourhood; the parents have already been seen and the general assessment is made

that the mother is rejecting the child and that the
father is hardly in the family at all. To begin with,
the interview with the child is diagnostic. It is
concerned with establishing or contradicting the
hypothesis that he is a deprived child. The hypothesis
is confirmed. The next question is, 'What should be the
disposal?' Different facts are now needed from the
child. He might well be asked if he has any favourite
uncles or aunts, and tactful questions could be put to
him to see if he would like to live with one or other of
them (although, of course, no decision could be made
about this without much further investigation). It is
discovered that there is nobody to whom he feels
attached. His anti-social behaviour is such that urgent
action has to be taken. It is clear that he will have to
go into the care of a social agency, at least temporarily.
The next fact to be discovered is how he would feel
about this. He rejects the idea.

Now at this point it would be possible to make this
disposal whether the child liked it or not. The original
objective of the interview – to find out the facts – has
been accomplished. However, an anti-social child will
probably become even more anti-social if he is pushed
around, so a manipulative type of interview will have
to be employed. The original interviewer may decide
to do this himself, or he may decide to leave it to
somebody else, such as the case-worker from the
agency concerned. If he chooses the latter, he does not
tell the child what disposal has been decided upon,
because to do so would arouse antagonism without
giving any opportunity for discussion; instead he
leaves the matter until it can be handled by the
appropriate person. Let us now suppose that the child
agrees with the disposal, in other words the manipulative interview has been successful. He will still have
doubts and reservations, however, and the interview

can become supportive.

It might be worth noting here that it is possible to get the information required, that is to carry out a 'successful' fact-finding interview, but in so doing antagonise the child to the point where it is much harder for any subsequent interviewer to make contact with him. This is an error made over and over again by police and other law-enforcement officers.

Magnetic 'fields of force' provide a useful analogy in understanding the dynamics of an interview. Imagine a compass on a table. Scattered around it are many magnets, some large and powerful, others weak; some are clearly visible, others are out of sight. The position of the compass needle will depend on the combined effects of all the magnets. If the compass is moved about, its needle will be deflected as its distance from the various magnets changes. When immediately over a weak magnet it may be more affected by that than by a more powerful, but distant, one. Pointing North can represent maximum achievement of the objects of the interview, and the magnets represent all the factors that help or hinder. Moving the compass is analagous to changing the topic under discussion. The interviewer has to keep the needle as close to North as possible, partly by adjusting the position of any magnets that are adjustable, partly by moving the compass into appropriate positions. Not all the magnets will be obvious to the interviewer. He has to infer their position, strength, and direction from the behaviour of the compass needle.

Four   Communication

Any interview is in a continually changing balance between the factors that encourage communication and those that oppose it. What is more, we have already seen that at any given point some type of communication will be encouraged, whereas others will be inhibited. A warm feeling towards the interviewer will motivate the child to communicate – fear, suspicion, or hostility will stop him from doing so; interest will help, boredom will hinder; an urgent desire to solve his problems will make the child want to talk about them, embarrassment will make him want to avoid discussion. The job of the interviewer is therefore to exploit those factors that increase communication (especially on the topics that are relevant) and minimise those that block communication. Communication includes both speaking and hearing, and the child will communicate only if, *on balance*, it is worth his while to do so. He must recognise that the interview is relevant to his problems, and that this includes recognising the interviewer as somebody who can do something about them. On the other hand he may feel that he stands to lose more than he gains by communication. For example, if he is in trouble at school, he may lose more than he gains by a confession that implicates his friends – the punishment that he suffers unjustly from the teacher may be less than he will suffer from his friends.

An adult usually takes part willingly in an interview, or at least he has no strong objection to it. (Exceptions are psychotics, who do not realise that they are in any way sick or abnormal, and criminals being interviewed by the police.) In many interviews with children this may not apply. The child himself may not have chosen to be involved in any treatment or counselling situation; he may feel strongly that there is no need for it at all. Even if he accepts that something has to be done, he may much prefer that somebody else was doing it. We have seen that he may start off with major misconceptions about the purpose of the interview and the intentions of the interviewer, and that these misconceptions may apply simply because nobody has bothered to explain to him what it is all about. What is more, he may have been actively misled. For example, a parent says to a badly behaved child, 'It doesn't do any good when *I* punish you, I am going to take you to the probation officer.' The probation officer may be an enthusiastic believer in non-punitive or non-directive approach, but after the mother's remark the child has no doubt that he is an even bigger and better punishing figure than the parents are.

All these misconceptions will block communication and should be discovered at the beginning of the interview. It is always worth asking the referring person what reason the child has been given for the interview, and what he thought about it. The answer one gets is often unreliable, but it might offer some pointers. The example was given of a child who is mistakenly expecting a 'needle' from the psychologist. If the interviewer chats about school and part-time activities, the child is anxiously wishing he would stop the nonsense and get the needle over with. The child may be prepared to accept a needle, but sees a conversational interview as a completely unjustifiable

intrusion into his private life. Under these circumstances, asking him personal questions will make him
resentful, and from where he sits the fact that the
psychologist wears a winning smile and uses his nickname is simply nauseating. Perhaps all this could have
been avoided by a simple explanation.

It is not enough to minimise the blocks to communication in general; we must maximise the factors that
facilitate the type of communication we want. Many
writers on case-work practice and similar types of
interviewing take it for granted that the patient or
client has some wish to communicate because he has
some problem he wishes solved. It is easy to overlook
the fact that this may not apply to a child because
children are used to doing what they are told by adults
and will come to the interview and answer questions
simply for that reason. A child in this frame of mind
will take no active part in the interview, and it will be
pretty unproductive. If the child is asked how he is
getting on at school, he may answer, 'Very well, thank
you' or 'All right, I guess' – from his point of view this
is none of the interviewer's business or, even if it is,
the child cannot see what he personally has to gain by
talking about it. It is therefore necessary to establish
that the interview has some relevance to his own
problems and also that the interviewer can do something to help him. To rely solely on warmth, permissiveness, and freedom from pressure might not be
enough. The child might feel at ease in the interviewer's presence and even feel quite friendly towards
him, but nobody discusses all his personal and intimate
problems with every friend he has. The children's two
principal attitudes to being interviewed can be shown
on a chart (Fig. 1, p. 28).

Tom has a problem, knows what it is, and wants help
with it. This places him at the extreme left-hand side

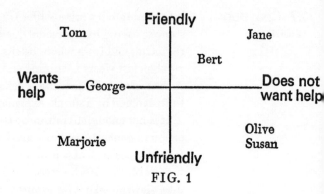

FIG. 1

of the chart. He feels friendly towards the interviewer, and would like him to be the person involved. This places Tom high up on the chart. Jane is just as fond of the interviewer as a person, but is opposed to having any sort of 'help'. She is, therefore, high on the chart, but on the right-hand side of it. George definitely wants help but is neutral in his attitude to the interviewer as a person, whereas Marjorie wants help, but dislikes the interviewer. Bert does not feel strongly on either point. He feels vaguely friendly, which places him above the horizontal line, but would rather prefer not to talk about his problem, which puts him slightly to the right of the vertical line.

The object of any interview (other than one that is frankly manipulative) is clearly to bring the child to the top left-hand corner of the chart and to keep him there. Unfortunately it may be possible to move him upwards, but not over to the left, and the interviewer remains what Redl and Wineman have called 'a friend without influence' (exemplified by Jane). Interviewers who are preoccupied with being warm, friendly, and accepting may overlook the lack of leftwards movement, and then be surprised when there is no change of behaviour outside the interview. This is shown in Fig. 2 (p. 30); Olive has become very friendly, but that

is all. The setting and approach for the interview will
be determined, to some extent, by the child's position
on the chart. If he is in Tom's position there is no
problem – they can get straight down to business in an
office. Marjorie, on the other hand, dislikes the interviewer, but she may be under so much pressure to solve
her problem (she is at the extreme left-hand side of
the chart) that she will co-operate in the interview.
If Susan is to be seen, though, the outlook is different.
An interview in an office, with no element of contact
except 'the problem', is bound to fail.

Susan can be approached in two ways – either
concurrently or consecutively. If we are unable to
move her up and to the left at the same time, we can
concentrate on moving her in one direction at a time:
we can concentrate on becoming friendly and ignore
the problem altogether for the time being because she
will move to the left more easily once she has begun
to move upwards (Fig. 3, p. 30). Alternatively, if there
is no time for this, it may be advisable to 'turn on the
heat' so that she is faced with a crisis and forced over
to the left. For example, if she is doing badly at school
and rejects all offers of help, she may move to the left
if threatened with expulsion. If she is running away
from home and sleeping around, one appearance in
juvenile court with a one month's remand may have
the same effect. If she then discovers that the interviewer is, in fact, providing practical help, she will
usually become more friendly (Fig. 4, p. 30). It is
obvious that the interviewer we are referring to is not
the one who should apply the pressure.

It must be remembered that our offers of help and
friendship may appear patronising and intrusive. If a
stranger were to come up to me in the street, point out
that I turn my toes out when I walk, and offer to
correct this, I would feel insulted and indignant. I

know that I turn my toes out and if that spoils his day I am sorry, but he does not have to watch. All too often this is how our approaches appear to the children we are trying to help. It is arrogant of us to assume that a child *wants* our friendship – we may have to work hard to persuade him that it is worth having. Many of the children we see do not want adult

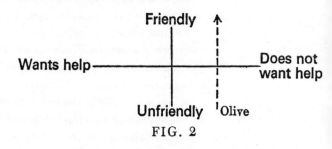

FIG. 2

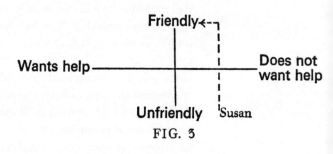

FIG. 3

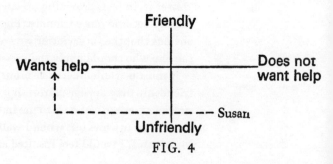

FIG. 4

friendship because they have been let down so often
in the past. Marjorie may be like this – but we can help
her by adopting a matter of fact, businesslike approach
(perhaps by tutoring her in school subjects or finding
her a place to live). She will accept our services, be
helped by them, but have no more feeling for us than
we have for the bus driver who gets us to the destina-
tion on time. So what? Are we trying to help the child
or to satisfy our own needs to be liked?

We must recognise the difference between 'the
problem with the child' and 'the child's problem'.
The difference was exemplified earlier with the
situation in which Johnny was quarrelling with his
sister (p. 10). Johnny's problem was his sister's
meanness, his mother's problem was the physical
attack. An interviewer may be caught in the middle
of a conflict between, say, a child and his parents.
The essential requirement in a situation like this is to
recognise the motivations and aims on both sides. I
know of one case-worker who wanted to work with
delinquent boys, but found himself unable to settle
into any agency. This was because he identified so
strongly with the boys that he could not, as he said,
'tell them the things society expects me to tell them'.
I do not think that this is a real difficulty; it is perfectly
possible to point out that society will react in certain
ways to the boys' behaviour without making a moral
judgement either way. In other words we can warn
children without threatening them. The position of
the interviewer may be that of an interpreter, not an
umpire – an umpire's decisions may be rejected by both
teams.

On the negative side, tending to prevent communication, is the fact that the child might not be merely
uninterested or unimpressed, but actively suspicious
and afraid. If he is in some sort of trouble, it is vitally

important to avoid identifying with the adults who are 'bugging' him by the use of critical remarks such as 'I see that you're not doing very well in school' or 'Your mother says that you have been very naughty lately'. It is possible to put the same point in a neutral way, such as 'I gather that things have not been going too well at school; I've heard what your teacher has to say about it, but I'd like to hear your point of view'. One can even be a little more encouraging without committing oneself to approval of the child's behaviour. If his foster-parents report that they cannot keep him any longer and a new place must be found, one can say, 'Mrs Smith tells me that things are not going too well. What is it that you don't like about the place?' This implies that not all the fault is on one side and that the child has every right to have complaints of his own. It is essential, of course, not to make this remark in a way that implies you are astounded that he could possibly dislike such a wonderful foster home, or vice versa.

It is sometimes a good idea to start by spelling out one's own obligations and intentions. One cannot expect the child to speak freely if he thinks that everything he says 'will be taken down in writing and may be used in evidence'. But to start off by assuring him that it will not, if the idea had never crossed his mind, will make him unnecessarily apprehensive. If he has reason to be apprehensive anyway, I usually start in this way (this is especially applicable if one is interviewing on behalf of the courts): 'Hello, George, my name is Dr Rich. The judge isn't too sure what to do about you and he wondered if I had any suggestions to make. I have to make a report to him, but as I am a doctor anything you tell me can be treated as confidential; you'll have to warn me, though, if you say something you want off the record, because other-

wise I might put it in the report by mistake.' If the
interviewer has the advantage of being a doctor, he
should cash in on the faith usually accorded the medical
profession. Even quite young children are often aware
of the fact that doctors will not give away their secrets
if asked not to.

However, to start off in this way with a child who is
not in any sort of trouble would imply that you believe
he is guilty of some secret sin or crime and that you
want to extract a confession from him. (The child is
undoubtedly guilty of secret sins and crimes, like the
rest of us, but they may be quite irrelevant to the
matter at hand.) At some stage, however, conditional
confidentiality must be promised. What these con-
ditions are depend on the interviewer's point of view
and on the circumstances. Even if the parents and
teachers are the kindest and best-meaning people in
the world, the child's *feeling* that they are likely to be
hostile or critical is what counts. On the other hand it
is possible for the interviewer to put himself in a very
difficult position by promising confidentiality. At one
time, when seeing a large number of delinquents,
I was kept informed of 'jobs' that were about to be
carried out by a well-known mob in South London.
As a good citizen I should have informed the police,
and by not doing so I became an accessory before the
fact and liable to prosecution. However, had I informed
the police I should immediately have lost all possible
chance of working with these lads and almost
certainly should have prevented anybody else from
doing so. It seemed to me that my larger duty to
society was to reform these characters rather than to
prevent one particular offence. However, this is a
matter that has to be decided personally by each interviewer. I have been frequently amazed at the amount
of dangerous and secret information I have been given

by both children and adults on the simple single statement that I would respect their confidences. This applied even when I worked for a prison authority interviewing men in custody. It should be noted that most of us have no protection from the law in these circumstances; the law recognises confidentiality for priests and lawyers, but not for doctors and other interviewers. In practice, however, if the interviewer is honestly trying to be fair to everybody, it is usual for his conflict of loyalties to be recognised and accepted. Judges and lawyers almost always understand the position he is in, although some police officers do not. They feel they are perfectly entitled to ask a social worker to trap a child into admissions that can be used in a successful prosecution. The police officer himself is in a different position. It is his duty to trap the delinquent child; the child recognises this and does not resent it unless, of course, the policeman does so by unfair means such as promising to keep a secret and then not doing so.

It is unfortunately true that the adult world tends to ignore children unless they are causing trouble. In other words there is always a tendency for a child being interviewed by a stranger to jump to the conclusion that the only reason for the adult's interest is because the child has done something wrong. (I once heard the porter on a train trying to be friendly with a young child. He opened the conversation by saying, 'Are you a good boy?' Would he have approached the child's mother saying, 'Are you a moral woman?') Even if the child does not have this defensive and cynical outlook, he still knows from experience that adults are liable to impose unwanted directions or restrictions upon him, and I think it is generally true that even the most trusting of children will start off by being rather defensive unless the interviewer is a

welcome one for the child – for example, when a
prospective Scout is being interviewed by the Scout
Master.

The problem of a conflict between loyalty to the
child and to his parents is subtle and difficult. Parents
are entitled to know, up to a point, all that is to be
known about their own child's activities. With young
children this covers just about everything; with
teenagers, perhaps only as little or as much as the
child himself cares to divulge. The decision varies
with the importance of the circumstances and the age
of the child. If a seventeen-year-old girl is pregnant,
her parents should know about it, although it is not
nearly so certain that they are entitled to know the
name of the boy or man concerned. If the girl has a
passionate desire to protect him, her present distress
will be made much worse if she is forced to give his
name.

My own rule of thumb is to ask myself why the
parents want the information they are seeking. If they
have a genuine desire to help the people concerned, it
is usually possible to persuade the child to give them
the information or to give permission for it to be given
by the interviewer. If, however, the parents are
simply being vindictive or nosy, I see no reason why
they should be encouraged in these bad habits. Of
course, even the best of parents will become resentful
if the interviewer does not explain his need to respect
the child's confidence on the grounds that this will help
everybody in the long run.

It is very important to note that *intending* to respect
the child's confidence is not enough. If he can hear
what is being said in the next room, it will be obvious
to him that the people there can hear what *he* is saying.
If he is left in a room with other people's files on the
desk, it may occur to him that his file will be similarly

accessible to other people. If he hears his interviewer discussing some other case, he could reasonably expect his own case to be discussed in front of another child. Actually, everybody working in the social-service field is guilty of indiscretions over and over again. It is impossible to avoid them unless we are constantly conscious of the danger. We must recognise that interviews do not begin and end when we think they do; they begin when the child first comes into contact with the interviewer and end when he leaves. If he is sitting in the waiting-room and can hear the interviewer talking on the telephone, the interview has begun even though the child's arrival has been unnoticed by the interviewer, who may be communicating vitally important facts (such as the way he treats other people). The regard for confidentiality must extend into the precautions taken by secretarial and other office staff. It is far better to err on the side of being over-discreet rather than to be even slightly careless. For example, Mary asks whether Jean (whom she has met in the waiting-room) is staying with her grandmother while on holiday. As far as one can tell, this is an innocuous and reasonable question, and there is no reason why it should not be answered perfectly simply. However, it is still better to say, 'You'd better ask Jean about that. I have a very strict rule about not talking about my clients to anybody else.' This can be said in a somewhat apologetic way, making it clear that you are not reproving the child for asking the question; the fact that you are being so punctilious is very reassuring to the child because she knows now that her own affairs will not be discussed either.

It will often be necessary to reassure the child when something crops up in the course of the interview. If the office is on the ground floor and the child keeps

glancing at the open window, it might be that he is
afraid he can be overheard; all that is necessary to put
him at ease is to close the window. If he appears
embarrassed, he should be reassured that he has no
cause to be. If he protests his innocence, he may need
to be told that no harm will come to him if he admits
his guilt – if, of course, this is the case.

If the child becomes anxious and hesitant, sometimes a simple expression of interest such as 'I see' or
'Uh huh' is all that is necessary to start him talking
again. An indirect warm expression of understanding
and sympathy is usually more effective than a cold
clinical reassurance that he has nothing to worry
about. But whatever one does, it is important to bear
in mind the basic concept that there is a balance
between those factors that increase and those that
decrease the motivation to communicate. Suppose the
child is embarrassed about a topic on which we are
questioning him. His anxiety can be diminished by
our saying 'I know it's tough to talk about it' because
this shows that we understand and sympathise with
his difficulty. It may be that he also wants something
to be done about the problem, and this motivation to
talk can be increased if we add '. . . but it will be
worth it to get this whole thing cleared up'. The child
will be even more likely to talk if he knows that this
particular interviewer is in a position to help him, so a
further addition might be made: 'When I know all
about it we can decide what to do next.' In short, there
is one factor reducing his wish to communicate
(embarrassment) and two increasing it (hope that
something can be done, and expectation that help is
available immediately). The interviewer's remark
should take all three factors into account.

In adult interviews, too, the balance can tip in
favour of, or against, communication at different points

during the session. But children are more unstable in
their emotional responses, more likely to be over-
whelmed by a single moment of antagonism or
enthusiasm. Once I was interviewing a child who had
always been friendly and co-operative; on this
occasion he was sullen and clearly resentful. For a long
time he would not tell me what was wrong, but
eventually he admitted that he was upset because I
had (quite unknowingly) timed the interview to
interfere with one of his favourite TV programmes.
He had not told me because he assumed that I would
think this of no importance. Although it played havoc
with *my* schedule, I apologised and released him
immediately. I was not spoiling him, just being
practical. I would have got nowhere with him in that
mood; in fact it might well have coloured our relationship for weeks. A point to remember is that I was
treating this boy, not bringing him up. My objective
at this point was free communication on his part. If I
had been his father or school teacher I might have had
other objectives, such as showing him that he must
learn to accept frustration, and I should not have
achieved these by letting him do as he pleased. On
another occasion, even as his psychiatrist, I might
have had this latter objective – what was good interviewing technique on one occasion would have been
wrong on another.

Reassurance can be non-verbal. An example of this
is to pass the box of tissues to the child when he is
trying not to burst into tears; this will indicate that it is
perfectly in order for him to cry and that you have
every sympathy. Nine times out of ten this simple
gesture will be enough – he will burst into tears and
will then be able to speak much more freely. When
a nine- or ten-year-old boy is in this position he may be
very embarrassed indeed about crying in front of a

stranger. In this case you should push the tissues
towards him and walk over to the window and look
out of it, tactfully not noticing his tears until his
sniffling has stopped. Then you should turn round
and continue as if nothing had happened. The child
will know that you know that he has been crying and
will recognise your tact as evidence of your understanding.

We now come to the much more subtle area of the
child's feelings for or against the interviewer as a
person. We have seen that these feelings are not
entirely within the interviewer's control, for the
child may already be highly prejudiced one way or the
other because of the interviewer's age, sex, or other
unalterable characteristics. Rogers[1] sums up the
requirements for a good relationship as follows:
(a) warmth and responsiveness, (b) permissiveness
with regard to expression of feelings, and (c) freedom
from pressure or coercion. In other words the child
must think of the interviewer and himself as 'we'
rather than as 'you and I'. It is evident that some of
these requirements may contradict other objectives.
No school principal can be completely permissive
about expression of feelings; nor, if he is trying to
persuade a child to take a certain line of action, can
he be said to be avoiding pressure or coercion. On the
other hand if he is trying to find out why a child is
doing badly in school, it is essential that he *does* allow
the child to express his feelings. It is therefore again
evident that the interviewer has to be very clear in
his mind about his immediate and long-term objectives. In an ideal world, in which we could spend as
long as we liked with any individual child, all
relationships would begin with the qualities described
by Rogers, because if the relationship between the

[1] C. R. Rogers, *Counselling and Psychotherapy*, pp. 87–9.

child and the adult is good enough, everything else follows – the child will more easily accept advice, encouragement, and discipline, and will give and receive information freely. In other words, forming a rapport is a prerequisite for anything other than the most superficial work.

Five   Words

It has been shown that much important communication can take place without words, but nevertheless they form the essential stuff of an interview and must be considered in detail. The right words can encourage a child to communicate and can convey accurate information, but ill-chosen ones may have the opposite effects. The interviewer is more skilled in the use of words than is the child, partly because he is an adult, but more particularly because they are his familiar tools. The responsibility for their proper use, and for understanding what the child means when they are used inappropriately, is the interviewer's.

The interviewer may have to play a large part in maintaining the conversation himself. He must also be prepared to change the subject if the child is becoming distressed, because most children, and many teenagers, do not have the verbal skills to get out of difficult situations and will often withdraw into an embarrassed or sulky silence. The problem then facing the interviewer is exactly the same as the one that faces a dinner guest when he sits next to a shy stranger. He has to draw her out by finding topics that she wants to talk about, but he must also be prepared to make interesting contributions himself without monopolising the conversation. It is an old saying that a bore is somebody who talks about himself when we want to talk about ourselves; it is also true that it is boring for the child if the other person will not talk at all. If your interests are limited, you can be thought of as a good conversationalist only when you are talking to people who share the same interests. I use the word 'interests' and not 'knowledge' because it is possible to be genuinely interested in many areas in which you have no knowledge. If a young scientist of ten wants to talk about the mating habits of salamanders, or an amateur courtesan of seventeen wants to talk about the mating habits of movie stars, it is no good saying 'Tell me more' if you obviously couldn't care less. Not only will a genuine interest in the child's own chosen field be of help with this child, but the more you can learn about salamanders and movie stars, the easier it will be to carry on a conversation with the next child who wants to talk about this subject.

If an adult's concept of the child's world is determined mainly by the points at which that world impinges on the adult world, he is liable to bring up the wrong topics. For example, many adults invariably start a conversation with a child by asking how he gets on at school. (They would not think of opening a conversation with a stranger at a cocktail party by asking 'Are you successful in your job?') Most children do not *want* to talk about school, but do want to talk about their leisure activities and hobbies. The interview should therefore begin with these rather than with school topics.

The key to successful communication is having a common ground with the child. Some interviewers interpret this as meaning that they should be childish and should pretend to have interests and an outlook they do not have. This is ruinous – children are quick to spot such a phony approach. It is not so much interests and preferences that are important, as an attitude to life. If a child says that he loves milk chocolate and the interviewer says that he personally prefers olives, they are still on common ground because the interviewer can get as enthusiastic about olives as the child can about chocolate – we can have interesting conversations with children even though our likes and dislikes may be very different. A child might not be able to understand how we can spend a whole evening playing bridge, but he could easily understand our spending a whole evening doing *something* we like, because that is just what he does himself. He may not recognise the common ground unless it is pointed out to him, but it is the interviewer's job to do this.

Adults often do not recognise common ground because of their assumption of moral superiority. One of the pervasive qualities of our adult outlook is that we have built up a hypocritical self-image that successfully fools not only our friends but ourselves. It is surprising how often an adult will give a self-righteous lecture to a child about lying when he himself has just refused an unwanted invitation by untruthfully pleading a previous engagement. He will tell a child how wicked it is to steal when he himself has been padding his income-tax returns for years. He will give the child a lecture on the immorality of trespassing and then drive home at ten miles an hour over the speed limit. The adult attitude might be more impressive if the child were as convinced of our superior morality as we are ourselves. The chances are that a child will see through our hypocrisy, and teenagers are especially good at doing this.

Common ground is established also by use of the child's language. The way some interviewers set about this is like the way in which some Englishmen try to make a Frenchman understand them better – they speak English with a French accent. Speaking another language fluently does not consist only in knowing the

words or even the idioms, but of knowing the connota-
tions and the subtle implications of the things that are
said. If the average American uses the word 'communist', he probably means a fiend in hardly human
form. If an Italian uses the same word, he may well
mean somebody who is a neighbour, a close friend
with whom he happens to disagree politically. Similarly
the word 'cop' is not necessarily a translation of the
word 'policeman'. If a young delinquent says 'cop', he
means something quite different from a school
teacher's concept of a policeman. Here we have to
know what the word means to the child, not what it
means to us; it will mean something different because
his experience has been different and often more
limited – a six-year-old who has had experience of
only one school teacher might say, 'I don't like
teachers.' It should not be inferred from this that he
has a problem with authority. He may simply be
generalising from the fact that his one experience
with a teacher has been bad through no fault of his
own. Once when my daughter was six she came home
from a party. I asked her if she had had a good time.
She said, 'Yes, lovely. Rosamund's house caught fire.'
This did not mean, 'I hate Rosamund and her
parents', because in fact she loved them all dearly, but
'Next time I have a party of my own, I want you to set
fire to the house because it's great fun.'

In formulating questions, then, we have to consider
the effect of the topic chosen and the effect of the
language we use. We also have a choice of open or
closed questions and direct or indirect questions.

A *closed question* is one that requires a straight
answer such as 'yes' and 'no': 'How old are you?' 'Do
you like your teacher?' 'What is your favourite sport?'
An *open question* is one that requires an essay-type
answer: 'What do you think of teachers?' All these

examples are *direct questions* because the child knows more or less what he is being asked. If you want to know if there is any conflict between him and his parents over the time that he gets in at night, you can ask him in a direct form. You can also ask him *indirectly*, often by the use of two questions separated by several minutes so that the question is not obvious. For example, you can ask in a general discussion on rules and regulations, 'What time do you think boys of your age should be in at night?' and later on, 'What time do you have to be in at night?' He may answer 'Ten o'clock' to the first question and 'Eight-thirty' to the second, and yet deny that there is any difficulty at home over this point if the question is put to him directly.

It is often possible to question a child indirectly about his parents and gain information that he will not give in answer to direct questions. You can ask children how they intend to bring up their own children when they have them. It is then usually easy to discover from their replies whether they approve of their own upbringing or whether they think they are going to make a better job of it than their parents did. In this approach it is important to make it clear that there are no 'right' or 'wrong' answers, but that you are asking for the child's opinion and that he has every right to one.

An insecure adult may modify his answers to conform with what he conceives to be the interviewer's opinion, or, if he is unsure of this, he may give an orthodoxly correct reply. The danger is much greater when working with children, because children always tend to feel somewhat insecure with a strange adult, and are afraid that giving the 'wrong' answer may get them into trouble. They are also familiar with classroom situations, in which most of the questions put to them are designed to find out whether or not they know certain facts, and not to discover their opinions. If the interviewer is interested in opinions, then, he must make it clear that the child will not be punished in any way or laughed at, whatever his opinion may be.

A *leading question* is not simply an important question as is popularly supposed. It is a question that suggests the answer: 'You don't like your mother, do you?' It is legitimate to use leading questions if it is clear what the child is trying to say and you are merely putting his thoughts into words, but they are, of course, dangerous because they may make him say what he does not mean. However, one way to avoid 'leading' the child is to give him a multiple choice. Many adults, and nearly all children, find it very hard to describe another person's personality, but they can choose from among a number of adjectives that are presented to them. It is important that none of the adjectives should sound derogatory. Asking the child 'Is your father strict?' or 'Is your father easy-going?' may be taken by him as an implied criticism and he may answer 'No' to both questions. If they are both put to him at once, so that he has to choose between them, he may find it much easier to answer because the implication is that all fathers are one or the other. He will usually find it easier still if you put it in this form: 'Compared with the fathers of your friends, is your father strict or easy-going?'

It is easy to be misled by children's answers because their frames of reference are different (an adult will often recognise that there are several frames of reference and will ask you which one you mean). If you ask a child whether he gets a 'good' allowance, he may answer in terms of what his friends get or in terms of what his parents can afford. Misinterpretation of a reply because of a different frame of reference also occurs in adult interviewing, but it has to be guarded against more carefully with children because their limited experiences makes their frames of reference highly unrepresentative. It is therefore necessary to ask children to elaborate on their answers much more frequently than adults.

It is evident that errors of assessment are more likely to occur when the questions are direct and/or closed, because if you are off-base the child has no chance to explain. On the other hand open questions may allow the child (intentionally or not) to avoid the point altogether. A good interviewer knows exactly when to use each kind and how and when to let the child off the hook by dropping questions altogether for a time.

For young children or for dull children it is important to put questions in concrete terms; for example, not 'What are your hobbies?' but 'What do you do in the evenings when you're not at school?' They may believe that 'hobbies' means 'handicrafts' and reply 'I don't have any', although in fact they do all sorts of things.

A useful concept in the structure of the interview as a whole is that of the 'funnel' or 'inverted funnel'.[1] In the funnel type of structure the interview begins with generalities. This has the advantage of minimising bias on the part of the interviewer; it also establishes the frame of reference. The interviewer can make the discussion more and more precise and concrete by gradually using questions that are more direct and more closed. The inverted funnel works the other way round. It is no good asking a child to answer questions about abstractions in an area that he has not fully thought out. If you do, he will probably be unable to answer at all or he will produce some orthodox

[1] See R. L. Kahn and C. F. Cannell, *The Dynamics of Interviewing*.

opinion. An intelligent teenager would be able to answer the question 'Are you ambitious?' whereas a child could not. One can arrive at the same conclusion with a child, however, by asking a series of specific questions about his hopes and plans for the future in a large number of areas, and if the general question is then put to him – 'Are you ambitious?' – he might well be able to answer 'I guess I must be'. We may make a faulty generalisation from replies that are specifically accurate because the child cannot conceptualise or has not yet conceptualised information we are trying to obtain. For example, a child may not be able to say 'I dislike the authoritarian personality', but, if asked which teachers he likes and which he dislikes, he will be able to say. If he is then asked why he likes them or dislikes them, he will probably be able to describe certain aspects of their behaviour. From this the interviewer can infer generalisations that the child himself is unable to make.

Inexperienced interviewers tend to structure the interview in one of two extreme ways. They may have decided on a list of points they wish to cover and insist on dealing with these in a predetermined order and ruthlessly refuse to be sidetracked. This is appropriate if time is short and the problem is superficial, but we have seen how apparently simple answers can be very misleading because the interviewer and the child are working in different frames of reference. To avoid this difficulty, some people go to the other extreme and recommend a completely non-directive approach. This allows the child to determine the topics himself with minimal guidance from the interviewer. In theory enough material will eventually be collected in this way for all the important facts to be gathered from it. This technique derives from psychoanalysis, in which there is a very good reason for allowing 'free associaion' of ideas in the client's or patient's mind. Unfortunately social workers have tended to adopt this approach uncritically, perhaps because of the successful evangelism of the psychoanalysts, perhaps because social workers, in striving to obtain professional status, have modelled themselves too closely upon a discipline that has already achieved this. I am not in any way denying the value of a non-directive approach when this is the appropriate one; it has subtlety, and can obtain information that is completely unavailable in any other way, but it does require a great deal of time and a special training, and is highly inefficient when a different approach is required. I knew of one social worker who was trying to work her way through college by selling from door to door. She had a natural ability to get on with people and rapidly formed a good relationship with strangers. However, she never sold anything. Partly because of instinct and partly because of her social-work training, every interview on the doorstep became a case-work situation. She learned a great deal about the housewives, but could not bring herself to carry out an efficient manipulative interview – which was necessary to sell the goods concerned.

Another example was given by a nineteen-year-old girl whose mother had developed schizophrenia. The mother would go to her daughter's lodgings and place of work, and accuse her of being a prostitute and a communist; the girl had to keep changing her home and her employment. She recognised that her mother was ill, but could not persuade her to go to a doctor. She asked for advice at the local clinic and saw a social worker. The conversation went something like this. *Social Worker:* 'I guess you must get pretty mad at your mother.' *Girl:* 'Yes, I do, I get absolutely furious, but I know she's ill, and it wouldn't help to hit her on the head.' *Social Worker:* 'I can understand why

you get mad at her. Tell me more about it.' This went
on for fifty minutes, culminating in the social worker's
saying: 'I expect it's helped to get all this off your
chest. Would you like to come and see me again?'
During the whole period the social worker had given
no practical advice. After her frustrating interview the
girl went to see a doctor who arranged for the mother's
admission to a mental hospital that evening, thereby
solving the problem immediately. Although both
these examples happened to involve social workers,
the inappropriately non-directive approach is not
confined to social-work practice, nor of course are all
social workers so naïve and unhelpful.

A similar, but opposite, error was made by a juvenile
court judge. A delinquent of my acquaintance had
been up before him on a charge of car theft. The lad's
background was complex, and he had many personal
problems. When asked by the judge what made him
commit the offence, however, he was not inclined to
go into all these details, so he said the first thing that
came into his mind – 'Just for kicks, I guess.' 'Oh,' said
the judge. 'Bored, eh?' There was nothing to reply to
this except 'Yes, sir'. 'A boy like you should have a
hobby. Have you ever tried bird-watching?' (The
judge was an enthusiastic bird-watcher.) 'No, sir.'
'You ought to try it. Would you like to?' At this point
the boy thought the judge was mad, but had nothing
to lose, he thought, by humouring him, so he said he
would. 'Good lad – the probation officer will help you
to join a club. You'll learn a lot, be out in the open,
much better than hanging around the street corners.'
So the boy duly took up bird-watching, in which he
had not the slightest interest, but, as he remarked to
me afterwards: 'If I take my eyes off them bloody
birds they'll have me up for a breach of probation.'

The social worker carried out a fact-finding interview when she should have been manipulating, the judge was manipulating when he should have been fact-finding. Every interviewer must be clear in his mind about what he is trying to do.

Generally speaking, a compromise between the two extremes of direction and non-direction is probably the best. Before starting an interview I usually make a list of the topics I wish to cover and then give the child a fairly free hand. The chances are that most of these topics will come up in one way or another and they can be dealt with in any order that appears natural; if one of them is not brought up spontaneously, there is nothing to prevent the interviewer from bringing it up himself. I also add to the list as the interview goes on – for example, when I would like the child to elaborate on a certain point, but do not wish to stop the flow of conversation.

It is useful to have a number of fixed points by which to measure a child's attitudes. In any institution, including a school, use can be made of one's knowledge of other staff members to assess the child's reaction to them. (It is of course important to recognise that these fixed points are not nearly as fixed as they might appear, because the way a staff member behaves in the common-room may be very different from the way he behaves in the classroom.) Similar use may be made of TV and radio programmes, books, and movies. A child who has a secret wish to be a bully is unlikely to admit to this in an interview. Very commonly, however, he betrays this by his enthusiasm for TV bullies. A warning must be put in here. A boy of eight or nine will often admire the athletic prowess of a movie or TV star, and completely ignore the personality the actor is portraying. In other words our inferences must be drawn from the things the child sees in a situation and not the things that we see ourselves.

There is no limit to the topics of conversation that can be used as a basis for inferences, and every interviewer must develop a technique of his own. Some of the questions I invariably ask are: 'Of all the people you've ever known in your whole life – relatives and friends – whom have you liked best?' 'What sort of people don't you like?' 'What's the best time you've ever had in your whole life?' 'What's the worst time you've ever had in your whole life?' 'If you could have three wishes – to have anything, go anywhere or do anything or change anything – what would you wish for?' I once made the mistake of saying to an unusually precocious nine-year-old boy, 'If a fairy came in the door and offered you three wishes, what would you say?' He replied sardonically, 'A fairy? I'd ask him if he thought I was a queer.' He was drawing my attention to the fact that he was not so young and innocent as he looked; in other words it required a rapid change of frame of reference. Somewhat similarly, I was sitting in on an interview in which a child said, 'I know a four-letter word beginning with F. Do you?' The interviewer got into a panic, hesitated and then said: 'Yes – five.' If he had looked the child straight in the eye and slapped either possible answer back at him, they would have got along well together. As it was, the interviewer's evident embarrassment and evasion led to a complete breakdown of communication: the child treated him with ill-disguised contempt from then on.

The 'three wishes' question can elicit revealing answers, but whatever answer is given must be elaborated by further questions to find out exactly what the child means by it. For example, if he wishes to have a ship of his own, it might be that he sees himself as a pirate captain or that he simply wants to get the hell away from everybody. He will also tend to give the orthodoxly correct answer to a question to begin with and may need pushing to give a truer one. A child who is rejected by and hates his mother will often select her as the person he likes best in his whole life. If we have evidence to show that he does in fact hate her, we should not question his answer, but should go on to ask whom he likes next best. This next answer may well give us a clue to the only period in his life when he felt secure. Further questions should then be put to see if his second answer has been given more or less at random. If, for example, he chose the foster-mother he had when he was seven, we can ask further questions about her. The way he describes her and talks about this home will make it clear whether he really did like her or just picked somebody out of the blue.

There may be two types of block to adequate communication. One is caused by the child's wish to avoid a certain topic; the other is a result of his inability to express himself – that is, the problem is intellectual, not emotional. Some ways of avoiding intellectual misunderstandings have already been seen: defining one's frames of reference, and not 'leading' the child by putting words into his mouth. If we are uncertain of his meaning we can use neutral phrases such as 'What do you mean?' or 'I don't quite understand'. It is important not to put all the blame on the child by implying that he is not expressing himself very well; it is perfectly easy to apologise for not understanding. If all else fails and it is still impossible to be sure what the child is trying to say, it is far better to give the impression of having under-stood him and change the topic and then come back to it later in some other way than to leave the child with the impression that he can't get his point across however hard he tries. With older children it may be possible to re-phrase the question when the answer is unclear, simply to ask for elaboration of a certain point, or to offer a summary of what you think he has said and ask if this is what he was getting at. It is particularly dangerous to do this with young children, who will quite happily agree to anything, and with any child or adolescent who is in a state of anxiety. Studies of brainwashing have shown that any person may develop an abnormal mental condition under stress in which he is highly suggestible. When in this state, even a non-leading but direct question such as 'Did you shoot the school principal?' may be enough to convince him (perhaps for several hours) that he had done so. The extreme forms of this phenomenon are not very common, but when they do occur they can be missed even by experienced investigators. What *is* common, however, is the way in which almost any child can be led, simply by the form of the question put by the adult, to make false statements. This is because their relative positions are unequal: the adult is so much more powerful and more sure of himself than the child. This imbalance will vary with the child's age, his personality, and his relationship with the interviewer.

So much for intellectual misunderstandings. In considering emotional blocks we must remember the concept of balance of factors in the interview. I have seen many transcripts of evidence from juvenile courts in which the judge was trying to find the facts, had been provoked by a remark made by the accused child, and had given him a lecture, thereby upsetting the balance of relationships, so that the child became much more concerned with defending himself from the judge than with remembering the facts about an event that took place some time before. This does not mean of course that a judge should never lecture juvenile delinquents. It does mean that, like any other interviewer, he must be quite clear in his mind about his immediate objective. And going after a secondary objective, however briefly, might make it impossible to achieve the first.

When painful areas have to be approached, one might use the analogy of trying to find a passage in a ship through a rocky channel. Some of the rocks are evident and can be avoided. The submerged ones can be foreseen by taking soundings and changing course when the water suddenly becomes shallow. By making a series of approaches from different directions, it is possible to map out the shallow areas and predict with reasonable accuracy where the dangerous rocks below the surface are. An interviewer uses the same sort of technique when he approaches each submerged problem from a different direction and in that way delineates the whole sensitive area.

Finally it must be emphasised again that the interviewer has a constant obligation to maintain the child's wish to communicate. There is no point in spending half an hour in building up a good relationship only to break it down by a series of painful questions or threatening remarks. If the other objectives of the interview are in conflict with the objective of improving communication, it may be necessary, from time to time, to abandon them. For this reason it is valuable to have a set of neutral or pleasant topics on which to draw at short notice if the going becomes difficult.

Six   Non-Verbal Communication

Even with older children and adults the actions that
accompany words are often very revealing. If there is
a contradiction, the action is more likely to be reliable
than the words. The younger the child, the more true
this is, partly because young children do not have the
verbal fluency to make their meaning clear. If we visit
a friend and he greets us with 'I hope you don't have
to rush away too soon', we take this as a compliment.
His five-year-old child might say, 'When are you
going?' This sounds quite different from what his
parent said, but may express exactly the same sentiment. Whether it does or does not will be indicated
by the child's expression and behaviour.

   Working with pre-school children is more akin to
animal training than to adult interviewing because
communication in each direction is in terms of
behaviour rather than words. The balance between
these two changes in favour of verbal communication
as the child gets older. Play-therapy techniques have
been derived to allow a completely non-verbal
conversation. I once interviewed a four-year-old child
whose mother complained that he had recently
become very hostile and difficult to manage and that
she could think of no change in the home situation
that would explain this. When I sat down beside him,
he was playing with some cotton-reels and a cardboard
box. After a few minutes' play, during which my
cotton-reel chased his cotton-reel and vice versa, I held

mine up and inquired, 'Who's that?' He replied,
'Mommy', and put her in the box. I asked 'What's she
doing?' and he said, 'Going to bed.' He then put
another reel in the box and I asked who that was. He
said, 'Daddy.' Thinking that maybe Freud was right
after all, I picked up another reel and said, 'Who's
this?' expecting him to say 'Me'. To my surprise he
said, 'Daddy', and put him in the box too. He then
picked up another cotton-reel and explained that this
also was Daddy and put *him* in the box. Fighting back
the thought that maybe Daddy had a multiple
personality, I decided that the child was just per-
severating (getting into a rut, which is very common
at this age), so I started playing a different game. A
few minutes later, however, he repeated the same
game with one Mommy and two Daddies in the box.
I then remembered that Father was frequently away
from home, so I went into the next room, having spent
a total of about ten minutes with the child, and said to
the Mother, 'You didn't tell me you had a lover.' This
wild guess came off. Her jaw dropped and she said,
aghast, 'Who told you?' I said, 'Johnny did', and in
fact this turned out to be the cause of all the trouble.
Never before or since have I had the psycho-dynamics
handed me on a plate in so rapid a fashion, but it just
goes to show how much can be said with cotton-reels
and a cardboard box.

Nobody would think of interviewing an adult and
arbitrarily limiting his vocabulary to five hundred
words. However, we often interview children, whose
vocabulary is movement and behaviour, and are forced
to limit these because of unsuitable surroundings. This
can be avoided by careful design of the room or by
conducting the interview outside the room altogether.
Most people interviewing children will have to do so
in a setting that is designed for some other purpose

R.I.C.

entirely, and even if this cannot be avoided we should at least recognise what the surroundings are saying to him. (Readers who are in the position to set up a room especially for interviewing children are referred to Appendix A in which detailed suggestions are given.)

Non-verbal communication begins long before the verbal part of the interview. In fact we 'say' a great deal to the child as soon as he walks into the room. One can go further back and recognise that the interview has begun when he first sees the building in which the interview is to take place. If it is a school or looks like a school, he will automatically fall into a pupil-teacher relationship with any adult he finds inside. If it looks like a prison he will feel threatened; if it resembles a familiar and friendly home he will be reassured. Apart from these general responses, probably made by most children, there is a wide variation of individual responses. For example, one teenager might immediately feel at home in an office in which the furniture consists of a couple of easy chairs, a rug on the floor, attractive drapes, and so on. Another might find this a threatening situation because it is too personal and would much prefer the neutral clinical atmosphere to be found with hard chairs and the interviewer sitting behind a desk. What is more, a setting or an approach that is conducive to one type of conversation or interview may be inappropriate and inefficient for another.

In looking around the room before an interview, then, we should ask the following questions: *What do I want my room to say to this child? Does this room say it, or does it say something else? What do I want the child to do when he comes in?* For example, a school principal interviewing a child who has been sent to him for repeated misdemeanors may intend to take a firm line, pointing out that if he persists in his behaviour he will be in trouble. A crude way in which the room could say this would be to have a strap laid prominently across the principal's desk. But if the principal's intention is to get to the bottom of the child's bad behaviour and he plans to approach him as an interested and friendly figure, then his best intentions and approaches would be completely spoiled if the child's eyes were constantly wandering to the strap. This is a crude and obvious example; a more subtle statement might be suggested by the position in which the principal places himself in relation to the child. If the interview is to be nothing more or less than a straight warning, the principal might sit behind the desk and have the child stand in front of it. In the more friendly type of interview he might prefer to set up a couple of chairs in front of the desk, or he might sit on the window-sill smoking his pipe, emphasising the informality of the proceedings. These points are so obvious that many readers may think they are not worth mentioning. However, we are all so used to our own surroundings that we frequently fail to recognise how they strike a newcomer. I have known many doctors to be puzzled by a child's evident fear while being examined, in spite of frequent reassurances that he is not going to be hurt, because they completely overlooked the fact that a number of ghastly instruments were in full view.

A point not to be overlooked is that everybody is most at ease in a situation that is familiar and expected, and as children's experiences are more limited than those of adults there are fewer situations or surroundings that they will find familiar. Because of this limited experience they also tend to see an adult not as a whole person but as a teacher or a policeman or a parent. Although one child may be more át ease in a living-room than in a classroom, he may still be more at ease with a teacher in a classroom than with the same teacher in his own living-room. It is not that the teacher (or the living-room) is unfamiliar, it is that the two in combination are incongruous and therefore rather worrying. It was pointed out above that the child may think of the adult as a teacher although in fact he is not one. If, therefore, this adult's behaviour and appearance are too dissimilar from that expected from a teacher, the child will become uneasy, although he would not be threatened by the same behaviour from the same adult if he met him on a beach or in a park. It can be seen from this that a greeting which is *unexpectedly* warm and informal may be disconcerting instead of reassuring – it is not always a good practice to rush at a strange child with one's hand held out and teeth bared in a welcoming smile. Even fairly sophisticated adult patients meeting in a group for the first time are often more at ease if placed around a table rather than around a room with nothing in front of them. So the child often feels safer if there is a desk between the interviewer and himself – and the interviewer is often safer too! With a younger child I like to start my own interview by sitting behind a desk and writing something. It is important to smile and call him by his name when he first comes in; then I usually say, 'Excuse me, I just want to finish doing this. Do you mind waiting a moment?' This gives him a chance to examine the room and to look me over.

A word must be said about the interviewer's clothes. Until they reach their teens children are not usually clothes-conscious, but something that appears to them to be grossly inappropriate for the situation or out of character for the person they think they are talking to can cause uneasiness. The teenager may base his or her

attitude to the interviewer and respond to him very
much according to the clothes he is wearing. However,
as with the words we use, the important thing is not to
imitate the child or the teenager, but to be consistent
and honest in the way we dress, not so much dressing
to create a particular effect, but recognising the effect
that we are in fact creating by the way we do dress.

The child is giving non-verbal information as well
as receiving it. Careful observation should be made
of his appearance, movements and changes of
expression. A list of the aspects of his behaviour that
can be observed is given in Appendix B.

If he leans forward or back, if he moves his chair
nearer or farther from ours or turns it so that it is at an
angle – these suggest approaches to or avoidance of
the topic under discussion. Interviewers should take
particular note of the feet, which the child thinks are
out of sight. The upper part of the body may appear
quite at ease, but his tension and anxiety will be
evident if he is curling his ankles around the leg of the
desk. The small muscles of the fingers and jaw often
give similar information. Tiny changes in the eyelids
are invaluable clues – a slight widening when he is
frightened and a slight closing when hostile or
thoughtful. Skin changes should also be observed;
these include slight flushing, pallor, and sweating.
The eyes will turn towards or away from the interviewer much more rapidly than the whole body, thus
indicating responses more immediately.

All this information is being poured out throughout
the whole interview. It will tell us not only the child's
general attitude to us and to the situation, but his
specific attitude from moment to moment as the
questions and discussion proceed. For example, the
relaxed position of his body may indicate that he is, in
general, at ease, although in response to one question

or comment from the interviewer he may suddenly
look away from what he is doing or his fingers may
pause momentarily from rolling a piece of plasticine.

We must, then, add another dimension to our
understanding of an interview. The child and the
interviewer give each other information not only by
their words, but by their appearance and behaviour;
and in addition the interviewer predetermines the
child's attitude to some extent by the surroundings in
which he conducts the interview. Some information is
given voluntarily, some is given unintentionally.
Ideally the interviewer would be aware of the effect
made on the child's mind by every word, gesture,
intonation and pause, and would recognise the
significance of everything the child does or says.

Seven   Modifying Factors

So far we have been discussing 'the child' as if there were an average or typical example. All the generalisations and suggestions that have been made must, however, be modified and adapted in the light of the following factors: age, intelligence, cultural background, previous relationship between the adult and the child, whether the interview is the first or has been preceded by others, and specific difficulties such as language or emotional disorder.

Age

It is not strictly true that there is a steady and regular increase in the importance of verbal communication as the child grows older. Commonly in adolescence there is such an extreme shyness that a completely verbal interview is far too threatening for teenagers, and it is necessary to hold the interview away from the office, in a far more behaviour-centred situation. For example, a teenager may be mute in the office, but talk freely while helping to decorate a club-room, service a car, or prepare a meal.

The limited and atypical frames of reference used by younger children have already been mentioned, and so has the fact that the younger the child, the more he will think and speak in concrete rather than in abstract terms.

Intelligence

The dull child of twelve with a mental age of eight does not speak and think like the normal child of eight who also has a mental age of eight. The dull child has more restricted interests and his thinking tends to be more concrete and specific. Interviewers should be on guard against the 'halo effect' of a dull child who looks bright or who talks a lot, thus often misleading even experienced interviewers. By the age of eight or nine dull children are often adept at changing the subject when they are out of their depth, or at answering brightly and enthusiastically when they really haven't the faintest idea what they are talking about. The interviewer can make a mistake in the opposite direction, by underestimating a normal or bright child who looks pretty dim, or who is unusually shy. The defensiveness of a dull child can be misinterpreted as sullenness if his basic problem is not recognised.

Cultural background

Attention has already been paid to the possibility that the interviewer and the child may attach different meanings to words. The ability of a child to express himself will depend not only on his age and basic general intelligence, but on whether or not he comes from a home in which there is a high level of verbal ability. A child from this type of home will (unless other factors are overwhelming) be much better able to express himself than children who have not had this advantage. On the other hand he may repeat statements he has heard at home without understanding them and mislead the interviewer into thinking that he has a greater grasp of a situation than he really has. This may in turn lead the interviewer to set the whole discussion at a higher level than it should be set with the result that, although the child will be able to keep his end up in the conversation, he will have to strain to do so, and the interview as a whole will not be so rewarding as it would have been if he had been treated at a more natural level.

65 Modifying Factors

Child's attitude to the interview

A child begins each interview with an attitude compounded of many factors. At the beginning of the first session he may be anxious or frightened or resentful or hopeful. His fears and doubts may be dissipated during the first few minutes, or they may persist for several weeks. If there is to be only one interview (as in much diagnostic work) stress must be laid on reassurance from the beginning, but if a series of meetings is planned the whole process can take place more slowly, and many of his anxieties might be ignored until a sound relationship has been built between the child and the interviewer. No interview begins quite where the previous one left off. The child has been leading his own life between sessions and he will bring attitudes to them that have been modified, to some extent, by the events of the intervening period. The longer the relationship between the interviewer and the child, the more stable it becomes, and the less it will be affected by these outside influences. The child may also have been thinking over something that was said to him during the previous interview, and so approach the topic in a different frame of mind; this can occur because the child had been persuaded to a point of view and abandoned it when the adult was no longer present to influence him.

Eight   Special Difficulties

One cannot decide how to deal with a difficulty in an interview until one knows what has caused it. If a child is acting aggressively, for example, you should not ask 'How should I handle the aggression?' until you have the answer to 'What has caused this aggression?' Has the child misinterpreted something the interviewer has said? Is he just a normally aggressive child? Is he defending himself against a real or an imagined threat? Another child may feel threatened, but respond with silence, excessively good behaviour, or complete withdrawal.

One cannot talk of 'difficulty' except in terms of the objective at any given moment. For example, anxiety or hostility inhibit free communication; in a fact-finding interview either one presents a difficulty. But if the interview is one in which the child is being told bluntly that his present behaviour will lead him into trouble unless he modifies it, then signs of anxiety may be taken as evidence that the message is getting across. Again, if the child has an anxiety-producing problem that he is anxious to solve, it dose not necessarily help him in the long run if the interviewer prevents the anxiety level from rising. This technique may simply permit the child to keep avoiding the problem and to use the interview situation as a welcome relief – a mistake commonly made by people who work with children because they want to be liked by children. (Even interviewers who do not have a

neurotic need to be liked are inevitably upset when
the child is upset – without some degree of empathy
they would not be very good interviewers.) Many
people think of the ideal interview as one in which the
child is happy, relaxed, and communicating freely.
They shut their eyes to the fact that there are times
when it may be necessary for him to be unhappy and
tense if the objective is to be achieved.

Successful interviewing really requires two contradictory attitudes. One is empathy in which the interviewer feels the same emotion as the child; the other
is a detached and scientific objectivity that enables
him to recognise the emotion and not be swamped
by it. Interviewers tend to have developed one of these
contradictory skills more satisfactorily than the other,
and they therefore differ among themselves in the
sorts of situations and relationships they find difficult.
Some are particularly good at supportive interviews
because they have great strength and courage on which
children can draw, but they do not respond very well
to the aggressively independent and rebellious child.

Many studies have shown that even expert interviewers force their own personalities on their clients
far more than they realise, and tend to push all
interviews into the same pattern without realising that
they are doing so. Perhaps the best we can do is to
recognise that we are more successful with one sort of
child than another, and to be aware of our own short-
comings even if we are unable to change them. One
way to gain this insight is to have some colleagues
watch an interview through a one-way screen or listen
to a tape-recording of it. They will inevitably notice
many occasions on which we missed the point or failed
to handle a situation properly because of our
prejudices and resulting blindness. Prejudice
by the interviewer comes under the heading of

'counter-transference'. Psychoanalysts use the term
'transference' to denote the emotion that a patient has
previously felt for somebody, usually a parent, and
that he transfers onto the therapist – responding to
him *as if he were* in fact the parent. Just as important,
but much harder to recognise, is counter-transference,
in which the therapist or interviewer responds to the
patient as if he were somebody else, or in response to
his own neurotic drives. For example, a man who has
unconscious conflicts about homosexuality and finds
it repugnant will often respond with hostility or
contempt if he is interviewing an effeminate boy; he
may be quite unaware why he is doing so and may
try to justify his attitude by seeking justifications for
his dislike.

To show the way in which any one form of
behaviour, such as aggression, can arise from a
number of different situations and therefore require
many different types of handling, it is worth considering the hostile attitude of an adolescent girl to a male
therapist. In the following examples it will be obvious
that some situations might arise at a first interview
only, whereas others would appear only in the course
of long-term treatment. They are given, briefly, to
demonstrate the wide range of possibilities.

1. Cultural differences between the therapist and
the girl may lead to a difference in their vocabulary
and their usage of words, and these could give an
impression of hostility where none was intended – the
interviewer considers a word insulting whereas the
girl uses it as a term of endearment.

2. The girl's antagonism to her father may be
transferred onto the interviewer.

3. She may have what is called a 'dependent hostile
relationship' with adults in general. This means that
she is dependent upon adults, but resents it. Her

increasing hostility towards the interviewer in the
course of treatment may indicate increased dependency
and may therefore be a good sign.

4. Many teenagers become hostile when they are
shy and defensive. With a male counsellor this might
reflect the fact that she is shy and therefore rude to *all*
men, or that she has a particular and personal regard
for the interviewer.

5. If the girl was deprived of affection as a child,
she may have given up all hopes of a positive relationship, and her attitude to everybody may be hostile
and aggressive.

6. She may be protesting reasonably against the
whole situation because she has been forced to attend
against her will – by a court, for example.

7. She may have a neurotic drive to provoke a
hostile response in other people. In other words she is
seeking punishment.

8. She may be 'testing limits'. Her hostile remarks
and acts are a way of defining the relationship and
assessing the interviewer to see how far she can go.

9. She may have a low tolerance for frustration.
Any interview contains frustrations, just as any other
situation in life, and it may be that the girl is simply
reacting to them.

10. If she is a Negress, a Jewess, an Indian, or a
member of any other identifiable group that is
commonly derogated, she may take it for granted that
the interviewer is prejudiced against her.

11. She may be responding to actual discourtesy,
tactlessness, or rudeness on the part of the interviewer.
(It is interesting that if one asks a group of experienced
interviewers to list the reasons that a patient might
be hostile, they will virtually never think of the
possibility that they themselves might have done
something wrong. At the most, they can recognise that

they might have mishandled a neurotic problem that the *patient* has.)

It is evident, then, that hostility may arise from her sex, age, race, colour, or class, the situation itself or something arising within it, or from her basic attitudes to people and to life, and have nothing to do with the individual interviewer or the particular situation. The question, then – 'How should I deal with aggressivity in an adolescent girl?' – is completely unanswerable unless all the factors in the particular situation are known.

Sometimes aggression is expressed in such a way that it must be controlled even though the cause is not obvious, or as an emergency measure while the cause of it is being investigated. (This is most likely to occur with younger children.) The essential thing here is to decide ahead of time how much aggressiveness will be allowed – what are the acceptable limits of various types of behaviour? These limits should be spelt out to the child and then strictly enforced. It may be decided, for example, by one interviewer that he will allow the child to throw paint at the walls, but not at him; another may allow the child to kick him, but not the walls. He may allow any amount of running around and shouting in the room, but none in the corridor. He may allow the child to burn paper in the fireplace, but not on the floor.

As soon as the child goes beyond the limit he must be stopped by whatever means are at the interviewer's disposal that do not involve punishment. For example, the door can be locked, the paints can be removed or, as a last resort, the interviewer can sit on the child. Even here, however, mere weight does not take the place of the right personality. Some people can use their hands to quiet a frightened horse, an angry dog, or an aggressive child whereas other people, who

appear to be doing the same thing, simply make the
situation worse. The essential difference seems to be
that successful 'handlers' indicate firmness and not
anger. If a child is trying to hit you, it is possible to
hold his wrists and to act as a dead weight to his
actions so that resistance increases as his fists come
nearer your body. This is completely different from
actually fighting him and trying to force his hands
back to his own sides. In other words the correct
technique is to resist the behaviour and not to
overcome the child. Incidentally, this is impossible if
the interviewer gets angry.

Many people – such as teachers who are in the habit
of interviewing children all the time, one way or
another – are often amazed at the amount of aggression
that the child psychiatrist or psychologist will accept.
The point is that the objectives of the two types of
interview are different. The psychiatrist is concerned
with finding out the total truth and with making
fundamental changes; the teacher is usually more
concerned with finding fairly superficial truths and
achieving relatively superficial changes in behaviour.
The teacher, however, is concerned with fundamental
changes in learning, with which the psychiatrist is
only incidentally and superficially concerned. In other
words the sort of behaviour that will help the teacher
to reach his objective may be completely different
from that which will help the psychiatrist to reach his.
The teacher may argue that he does not usually have
any difficulty with expression of aggression by a child
who may be much more violent in the psychiatrist's
interview. The difference lies in the fact that the total
structure of the classroom situation and the limits
tacitly accepted by both child and teacher make it
impossible for the child to express his aggressive
feelings in any overt way – all he can do is retreat into

sullenness or withdraw in some other way. At least an outward show of respect is necessary between teacher and pupil, but this is not needed at all in a psychiatrist's interview.

It is possible to overcome one difficulty in an interview while creating far greater difficulties in some other aspect of the relationship. This is why recommendations made by some psychiatrists to teachers about the way they handle a disturbed child – for example, that the child be given as much individual attention as he wants or that he be allowed to work at his own speed – are completely impracticable. These psychiatrists are concerned with a therapeutic effect; the teacher has a different objective – teaching. If the psychiatrist's recommendations were to be carried out, they might create a better therapeutic relationship between the teacher and the child, but they would interfere with the teaching relationship, not to mention the relationship between the teacher and the other children in the group, which would be affected by her change of relationship with the disturbed child.

After aggression, the most common difficulty likely to be encountered is silence and withdrawal. Of course these two words are not synonymous, for it is possible to have a perfectly friendly silence, either while the child is thinking over something the interviewer has said or is happily occupied in doing something with the interviewer or with the interviewer in the room. The child withdraws because he finds the interviewer threatening. The technique to deal with withdrawal, therefore, involves demonstrating in any way possible that the child can communicate with the interviewer without exposing himself to attack. This might be achieved simply by concentrating on neutral topics or by finding one in which it is worth the child's while to co-operate, perhaps simply by inviting the child to

take part in some activity that pleases him. This
approach cannot be hurried. A child will never settle
down to any activity if it is evident that the interviewer is sitting on the edge of his chair waiting for
the first opportunity to 'get back to business'. (It is, of
course, just as much the business of the interviewer to
improve communication as it is to do anything else.)
This technique can be carried on for too long; the child
may make a sort of unspoken bargain with the interviewer, and he is quite prepared to be friendly and
talkative so long as they don't talk about the important
matters. One cannot give any strict rules; all one can
do is recognise the constantly changing balance
between the factors that inhibit communication and
those that encourage it. The breakthrough may come
after many weeks, when the interviewer has demonstrated beyond all doubt that he is quite a nice guy
after all. On the other hand it may come suddenly
when the child is feeling particularly relaxed after a
violent game. Whenever the interviewer moves in,
however, he must be prepared to leap out again if or
when the child's resistance starts developing. Pre-
mature or over-insistent probing in the sensitive area
can undo weeks of hard work. Adolescents are
especially prone to sullen withdrawal, and this is one
reason why many interviewers find it extremely hard
to work with them, but exactly the same rules apply
to them as to younger children. Little can be done to
reach a withdrawn child if the interviewer insists on
working in an office and confines himself to verbal
interviews; 'play' therapy may be just as important
for the teenager as for the pre-school child, the
difference being only that the activity with the teenager is much more sophisticated.

Intelligent adults will often keep an interviewer at
bay by impersonal intellectual discussion of the situa-

tion; for example, a Jew who is suffering from anti-Semitic persecution may discuss this in every aspect except his own personal response to it. On the whole, children do not intellectualise until they become teenagers, but then they may use the technique extensively. Incidentally, one has to be on guard against interpreting genuine intellectual curiosity and excitement as an evasion of the point in hand. Just as a nine- or ten-year-old boy may get a lot of pleasure from pitting his physical strength against that of an adult, so a teenager will get pleasure in flexing his intellectual muscles. If the adult interviewer refuses to take part in an intellectual struggle, the adolescent may feel humiliated, because it appears that the interviewer does not think he is worth arguing with. The discussion itself may be completely irrelevant, but it will improve the child's self-image, and this is one of the motivations for communication.

Some children use appeal and seduction very effectively against susceptible adults. If a little girl is lonely, miserable, and frightened, sometimes the only effective thing to do is to pick her up and cuddle her. Having done so, you may find that she is adept at bringing tears to her eyes whenever in difficulties and that she has successfully manipulated you. A much greater difficulty arises with adolescent girls. All human beings, adult men and women as well as children, need to be picked up and cuddled occasionally, whether they admit it or not. There are some fourteen-year-old girls that a male therapist could and should pick up and cuddle in the same way that a nursery-school teacher comforts a four-year-old on occasion; but there are other fourteen-year-old girls who would call the cops as soon as he did so. The difficulty arises not so much because the therapist misjudges the girl's emotional age, but that her

emotional age can change in a matter of seconds from
that of a child to that of a young lady. In our society
boys do not take to being cuddled nearly so easily as
girls; the equivalent here would be an arm around the
shoulder, but even this can appear to have a homo-
sexual connotation. The cautious therapist plays it safe
by avoiding all body contact between himself and his
patients, but by doing so he loses an enormous amount
of communication that cannot be achieved in any
other way. Even so, the inexperienced interviewer
should be particularly cautious in this respect, because
the situation can rapidly get out of hand.

We have seen that because the interviewer is an
adult, especially an adult with high status or authority
in the community, he is at a certain disadvantage with
some children. On the other hand his words, recommendations, and support will carry more weight. If the
relationship is a good one, the child may well ask the
interviewer's own opinions or advice. A difficulty
arises in this situation only if the interviewer is not
clear what his objectives are. If he is carrying out a
fact-finding interview, the more he gives of his own
opinions the less he will be able to find out about the
child's. If the interview is supportive or therapeutic,
however, it may be that some firm recommendations,
or even flat contradictions of the child's opinions will
be invaluable. Even here difficulties do arise, because
the advice the interviewer gives may contradict that
given by the child's parents.

A particularly poignant difficulty arises with
deprived children. They have such a desperate need
to be accepted and understood that they may form an
intense relationship with the first person who offers
affection, whether this be a psychiatrist, a teacher, a
minister, or the man in the local store. The likelihood
of an intense response from the child is particularly

great with a skilled interviewer because he sets out deliberately to create this atmosphere of acceptance and understanding. Although the interviewer may take it for granted that his acceptance and understanding runs from 10 a.m. to 10.50 on Mondays, the child may assume that they will be available at all other times of the day and night. If this child then turns up at the office when the counsellor or interviewer is engaged in being accepting and understanding with somebody else, the first child may feel betrayed. There is no real answer to this problem; as with so many others the most we can do is be aware of it. The problem also arises to some extent with any adult who is in need of acceptance and approval, but he at least has an *intellectual* awareness that the therapist has other obligations. The child may be unable to recognise them and may feel that all the fine talk during the interview was so much hypocrisy.

A detailed consideration of the difficulties arising from various emotional disorders is beyond the scope of this book, but an explanation of some common mental defence mechanisms would be in order. One of these is 'projection'. This can be understood by thinking of the first time a puppy sees himself in a mirror. He may try to play with the other puppy or bark at it, not realising that it is to himself that he is responding. A hostile child will often project his hostility onto the world around him, and instead of saying 'I hate you', he believes and says 'You hate m (Note that this is not the same thing as a real hostility on the part of the interviewer that is engendered by hostile actions on the part of the child. In projection *all* the emotion is on the side of the child.) Another mechanism is 'repression', in which one forgets painful memories. It has been shown that some people tend to remember their past successes and others their past

failures. However honest we try to be, we all give
selected facts and a modified version of the truth, even
though this does not necessarily improve our public
image. A teenage girl who is very low in self-esteem
will simply not hear, let alone remember, compli-
mentary remarks, whereas the slightest criticism – or
a comment that could be taken as criticism – will
immediately catch her attention, and will be worried
about, remembered, and quoted. It is pointless to tell
such a girl that she gives a one-sided account of the
situation. She is speaking the truth as she sees it.

'Acting out' is another difficulty that should be
mentioned. Just as a child's total attitude and prejudices
for and against people outside will be reflected in his
attitude and response to the interviewer, so will his
response to the interviewer tend to be reflected in his
behaviour outside the interview. He will demonstrate
this attitude wherever it is safest to do so. If, for
instance, he hates his father, but is too afraid to show
it, he may transfer this hatred onto an adult male
therapist and, not being afraid of him, attack him.
Conversely, the interviewer may attack the child in
one way or another and make it impossible for him to
retaliate. I am not suggesting that the interviewer is
likely to whip him, but he may hurt him far more
deeply by criticism or humiliation. If the situation is
such that the child cannot answer back, he may 'act
out' this resentment against some innocent person in
his environment. This fact is well known to psychotherapists, who always have to beware in an interview
of stirring up emotions that cannot be successfully
dealt with and worked out at the time, but which spill
over and are expressed in all sorts of undesirable ways
in the world at large. The essential freedom of
expression inherent in a therapeutic interview,
however, makes this danger minimal. The danger is

much greater in a more rigidly controlled relationship – between teacher and pupil for instance, or policeman and suspect. It is apparent that a 'successful interview' is one that not only achieves its immediate objectives, but does not create other and worse problems outside the interview itself.

This leads us to the final point: that some difficulties may arise in an interview, not because of anything the interviewer says or does, but because of something that has happened since the previous session about which the interviewer knows nothing at all. This problem arises to some extent with adults, but it is more noticeable with children because adults are better able to remember more clearly what went on in the last interview and can separate off much more easily than the child can that part of his life that has been spent in a series of interviews. This is demonstrated by the frequency with which younger children, in a moment of forgetfulness, will respond to a psychologist as if he were a teacher, and still younger children will speak as if the interviewer is completely familiar with everything that happens in the child's own home. This means, for example, that if the child has been particularly naughty, he will arrive at the next interview expecting that here, too, he is in trouble, and this will modify his behaviour in a very confusing way.

Nine   Assessment and Recording

It is often very embarrassing for experienced and
apparently expert interviewers to have their interviews and assessments checked by others. It is
surprising how often they draw completely different
conclusions. The only reason most of us think that
we are good is because we never have the opportunity
of having somebody else check our results. In my own
assessment of a case I put far less emphasis on the
interview itself than on a detailed history and the
results of objective tests. Some experienced people
prefer to carry out their interviews without background information to avoid prejudice. I have reached
the conclusion that this approach is so unreliable that
it is completely worthless. However carefully the
interviewer has avoided the pitfalls that have been
mentioned so far, the fact still remains that all he has
seen is the child's behaviour in a particular situation
or a series of similar situations. The one factor that
these situations have in common is one of overriding
importance, that a particular interviewer is present.
A child may behave completely differently and say
quite different things when alone with an interviewer,
when with the same interviewer in a group of his
own friends, and when the interviewer is apparently
not present. All this leads to the conclusion that the
interview can be considered as only one part of a total
investigation, and a not very reliable part at that. It is
merely personal vanity that leads us to put such great

store by it. The same argument applies to interviews
that are supportive, persuasive, or therapeutic, instead
of investigatory. We like to think that the one hour a
week a child spends with us has as much if not more
effect on him than ninety-nine other waking hours and
all the other people in his world. Interviewing, however
highly skilled, is not the complete answer to anything.

The diagnosis and formulation, then, should not be
based on the interview alone. Its emphasis should be
on the aspect of the child or his behaviour that is
relevant to the purpose of the interview, but it should
not be overlooked that this cannot be understood except
within the total picture. If the teacher complains that
John is not working up to capacity, the counsellor
might interview him and find that he has no interest
in school work and might, on the strength of this,
recommend that he be allowed to leave school and go
to work. If he went into it a little bit farther, (as most
counsellors do) he might find that John has no interest
in anything else and will evidently be as unenthusi-
astic about a job as he was about his lessons. Even this
does not take us very far, and we need to know whether
this was a recent change in John's outlook or whether it
has always been the same. We need to know whether it
arises from trouble at home, preoccupation with a
particular personal anxiety, or perhaps even from
chronic undernourishment. It is not unusual to be
given a 'history' by a social agency that has had a child
in care for ten years and that gives dates of all his
innoculations and page after page of details about his
clothing, the addresses of his foster homes and so on,
but that gives us no information at all about the child
himself. When a child is thought of as delinquent, we
are often given a list of his delinquencies; if he is
considered disturbed, we are given a description of his
abnormal behaviour. Neither his delinquencies nor the

abnormal behaviour is the child himself. It is just as
important in each case to know the good things about
him as to know the bad ones.

Ideally, then, the more we know about any child
before an interview the more effective the interview
is likely to be, whether we are trying to stimulate a
child's interest in French, improve his moral principles,
or find out about his spare-time activities. This is not
less true because many people (such as teachers) have
to work with children about whom they know little or
nothing when they first meet them.

The next point to consider is assessment of the
interview itself. It was pointed out at the very
beginning (p. 3) that one of the essential elements of
any interview is feed-back – the child's responses
determining the interviewer's next move – and this
obviously requires a moment-to-moment assessment.
In making this assessment the following points should
be noticed.

*1 Spontaneous
remarks*

No remark made by the child is ever completely
spontaneous because the surroundings and behaviour
of the interviewer have conveyed a great deal before
a word is spoken. Even so, the less we intrude upon and
dominate the situation the more valuable and instruc-
tive the child's remarks will be. It is well known to
psychotherapists that the first few points brought up
by a patient in the course of any interview are sometimes the most significant, even if he immediately
changes the subject and does not mention them again.
When working with children we must of course
recognise that their spontaneous actions and behaviour
often take the place of spontaneous remarks by adult
patients. Attention should also be paid to the child's
behaviour 'after' the interview. It is by no means
unusual for a child to remain defensive and evasive

throughout the interview and then to loosen up when
he thinks it is over. This situation can be created
deliberately by the wily interviewer; he can put his
pen away and shut the file, walk over to the window
and make some remark about the weather, whereupon
the child may start to talk about all the things he has
flatly refused to discuss before.

*2 Contradictions
between physi-
cal responses
and verbal
responses*

In assessing the importance of a remark made by the
child, the interviewer should note whether his
behaviour is consistent with the sentiment expressed
or whether it is contradictory. Some of the points to
look for were mentioned on pages 61–2, but improved opportunities for observation are given if the
child is working with his hands while the talking is
going on. If, for example, he is explaining how dearly
he loves his teachers while pounding a plasticine man
flat on the desk, one rather doubts the accuracy of his
statement.

*3 Association
of ideas*

This is immensely important. If the interviewer
imposes his own structure on the interview, the very
valuable information given by free association will
never be gained. Quite often the child will give
himself away when he thinks he is changing the
subject. For example, he may evade discussion of his
attitude to a certain situation and then say, 'I saw a
good movie last week', and proceed to describe the
situation in terms of the movie story or one aspect of it.
What has happened of course is that thinking of the
situation, although not talking about it, has reminded
him of the movie. It is commonly found that a new
point raised after a comparatively long silence may
be a lot more closely associated with one immediately
preceding it than appears at first sight. Of course a
change of subject may be real as well as apparent, but

83 Assessment
and Recording

it should be noted whether this is due to boredom
with the old topic, to defence against it because it is
getting painful, or is caused by some external stimulus.

*4 Recurrent
themes*

If left to himself the child will probably keep coming
back to the same topic either within one interview or
over a series of interviews. This may show preoccupation with one person or perhaps with one situation
involving different people. It is not unusual for this
recurrent theme to be presented rather subtly and
not to be evident until one looks back over the notes
of several interviews.

*5 Evasions and
contradictions*

The experienced interviewer has a whole lot of pegs
in his mind on which he can, as it were, hang the
various points that have been raised, so that he can
keep an eye on them all at once. Later in the interview
something may be said that contradicts something
which was said earlier, or may tend to support a hint
that was not very impressive at the time. It should be
noted that contradictions may simply be due to slips
or to a faulty memory, or they may be due to a faulty
memory on the part of the interviewer or to a misunderstanding of what was said before.

*6 Provocative
stimuli*

The interviewer will set up a series of provocative
remarks to see how the child responds to them. By
'provocative' I mean remarks that are designed to fire
off a trend of thought or associations. A good hostess
at a dinner party or a good moderator of a panel uses
a similar technique when he or she drops a few words
into a silence and then sits back while the rest of the
group chase after them. The object of the hostess will
probably be merely to keep the guests talking, but the
object of the interviewer will be more specifically
directed towards a certain topic.

Opinions differ about the value of recording in the course of the interview. Some people feel strongly that note-taking inhibits the child and prevents the interviewer from given him his full attention. My own view is that the value of a record far outweighs the disadvantage. Over and over again I have read back my notes on an interview and have spotted things that I completely missed at the time. It is possible to miss the significance of points even if one has written them down; and in any case the record one makes oneself is likely to be selective and confined to those things one has noticed. With practice it is possible, by using a personal shorthand, to achieve an almost verbatim record. It is essential of course that one's own remarks be noted as well as the child's, and possibly significant movements should also be included – for example, that the child got up and walked about the room at a certain point although the reason was not apparent. A later reading of the notes may show that one had been working up to an area of stress and the child was finally provoked into movement. This happens because the interviewer can be so preoccupied at the time with the obvious content of the discussion that he misses the hidden content. It is also useful to look back over earlier interviews in the light of later discoveries. A lot of material that seemed unimportant at the time now stands out as being very significant.

I have said that one writes down only what one sees and hears. This problem can be largely avoided by the use of a tape-recorder, but the disadvantage of this is that it takes fifty minutes to listen to a fifty-minute interview, thereby doubling the time spent. However, there is no better method for improving one's technique, especially if the tape is played over to colleagues who are doing the same sort of work. Even the tape misses movement, and will not show how the child may have been 'led' to agree with a comment – not by the content of the remark itself, but by the way in which the interviewer looked up and smiled as he made it. I completely disagree with people who say that a tape-recorder necessarily inhibits a child. It is far more likely to inhibit the interviewer, especially if he knows he is going to play the tape to his colleagues. If the tape-recorder is set up as a matter of course at the first interview, the child comes to accept it perfectly naturally. A lot of time may be wasted to begin with because he wants to hear his own voice played back, but this is time well spent in motivating him to enjoy the interview. (It is important to make a special recording to be played back and not to let the child hear the interview itself, because he may be quite disconcerted by what he has said and this will probably inhibit further communication.) My own view is that it is unethical and immoral to tape-record anybody, regardless of age, without his knowledge. I always have the tape-recorder out of sight because the revolving spools are sometimes disconcerting, but I have the microphone in full view and I begin by asking the child if he minds if I use it. This should be done casually: 'I always tape record my interviews, it saves taking notes. I hope you don't mind?' If the child says he does mind, I switch the recorder off, but I have found objections to be extremely rare. It has been argued that some children object, but do not like to say so. This is a point worth considering, but even those who hold this view have usually agreed with me, after hearing the tape, that there is no evidence of inhibition due to the recording. A difficulty arises with children that does not occur with adults; a child is likely to roam all about the room. This means that one has to have a microphone that is specially

selected and placed to record anywhere in the room,
or to be satisfied with a less-than-perfect recording.
It is simply not worth trying to get the child to sit still
so that you can get a good tape.

Although tape-recording does present difficulties,
any means at our disposal to increase the value of
interviews, either by improved technique or by
improved assessment of what is said and done, is well
worth the effort. If one is setting up a discussion group
on interviewing techniques, based on tape-recordings,
it is as well to allow about two hours for every half-
hour on the tape. This is because it is most valuable
to stop the tape every time one of the group has a
comment or a question. The man who conducted the
interview ought to be able to justify every remark
he made, or every silence he allowed to develop, and
the choice of every word he used. It is also interesting
to stop the tape and ask the people present to predict
what is going to happen next, or how *they* would
handle a situation that has developed.

Even if an interview is not submitted for criticism,
it is still essential, if one is to have any justification for
thinking one's inferences are valid, to make a brief
summary at the end of each interview saying what
has been achieved and what is predicted. One must be
prepared to check these assessments and predictions
with scrupulous honesty against what actually
happens. I remember talking to the superintendent of
one penal institution for delinquent lads who told me
with great satisfaction of the effect that his final
exhortatory lecture had on the inmates. He said,
'Pretty well every boy who goes out of this room is
determined never to come back.' The fact that a very
large proportion of them actually did come back had
had not the slightest effect on his self-satisfaction. He
still thought that his final interview was highly

effective, although in fact there was not the slightest
evidence that it made any difference at all.

This, then, is the final point I would like to make.
Interviewers all too seldom ask themselves the vital
question, 'Does it work?' No matter how carefully you
have planned your questions or designed the furniture,
no matter how friendly you are, how much personal
analysis you have had to iron out your own neurotic
counter-transference, you are wasting your time
unless you can prove that the information you are
collecting is accurate, that the children you are
selecting for particular responsibilities live up to the
expectations, and that their behaviour does in fact
change in the intended direction.

Ten   Imaginary Interviews

These imaginary interviews have been prepared to
illustrate some of the points made in the foregoing
chapters. The material and comments have been
deliberately simplified; a genuine interview is so
complex that there is room for considerable discussion
and disagreement about the implications of the
remarks, and on how the interview might have been
conducted. In reading these examples or in studying
a real interview the essential is to make an active,
critical assessment instead of adopting the passive
acceptance that is normally brought to a play or a
movie.

Interview A

A well-meaning aunt is entertaining her hippie
niece at tea. The room is expensively furnished,
extremely tidy, and spotlessly clean; there are several
tasteless paintings bought at the local department
store. The niece feels that literature began with
Salinger and that Andy Warhol is an Old Master.
Her reaction to this setting is a mixture of
embarrassment, contempt, and sorrow. Spending
her time with a group of friends who are trying to
work their way through college, and frequently have
too little money to spend for food, she resents the
rather ostentatious wealth that surrounds her.

AUNT: *Well, Ginny, it's nice to see you again.*

The niece's name is Virginia, and she has not been
called Ginny since she was a child. It is felt by her

friends that even Virginia is somewhat of a misnomer,
and they invariably call her by her nickname instead.
Virginia's response to this opening remark, then, is
already complex. To some extent she reverts to being
'Ginny', but part of her resents her Aunt's not noticing
that she has grown up.

AUNT: *I made some cucumber sandwiches for you.*

These used to be a great favourite of Virginia's and
it is a long time since she has had afternoon tea, let
alone cucumber sandwiches. She immediately recognises that her aunt is making a great effort, and is
very touched by her remembering this old reference.

VIRGINIA: *Oh, how lovely. I haven't had these for
years.*

Her pleasure and evident sincerity delight her aunt,
and for a few moments they get on well together.
During a friendly conversation the following remark
is made.

AUNT: *Do you have a young man?*

This question throws Virginia completely. It is true
that she is living with a penniless artist called George,
but this is only a temporary arrangement. Knowing
that her aunt would be shocked to the core if she
explained the situation, she takes refuge in flippancy.

VIRGINIA: *Oh, I have lots of young men.*

AUNT: *No special one? I was engaged to your uncle
when I was your age.*

Virginia is not sure whether to take this as a reproof,
but remembering her aunt's evident pride in the somewhat inadequate husband, she decides to tease her aunt.

VIRGINIA: *I'm sure you had lots of young men simply
flocking around you before you picked on uncle.*

Aunt is rather pleased with this remark and smiles
reflectively. Virginia notices the smile and says quickly:

VIRGINIA: *I knew it. You should see the way you're
smirking.*

R.I.C.

She has thus neatly turned the discussion away from her own affairs to those of her aunt, and pays the price of having to listen to reminiscenses that are not really of great interest to her, but that are better than embarrassing questions.

AUNT: . . . *and you should have seen the parties we had.*

Now Virginia's group rather pride themselves on their parties, and she feels that her aunt is implying that the younger generation does not know how to have them.

VIRGINIA: *Don't think we don't have lots of parties too.*

This defensive remark was a mistake, because it redirects aunt's attention to Virginia.

AUNT: *So I hear. And from what your mother tells me, a lot of drinking goes on.*

This comment was unfortunately phrased. In point of fact Virginia's group cannot afford to drink much, and they indulge in cheaper pleasures. However, the critical tone of the remark upsets the girl and she feels estranged again and also a little guilty, so she changes the subject and hits back at her aunt's furnishings.

VIRGINIA: *Not really. You know I've always been intrigued by that picture over there. All those ladies standing around wearing draperies . . . do you think they're waiting for a bus?*

AUNT: *At least you can see they're ladies, which is more than you can say for some of the things that Picasso paints.*

From this point on they bicker about art – neither hoping to convince the other – and each feels frustrated and misunderstood.

Interview B

A youth-club leader is interviewing one of the local tough guys who he hopes will join the club. When Johnny 'Flash' Jones walks in, the leader has to decide immediately which name to use. Resentment might be caused by using his nickname without invitation, but he decides to do so.

LEADER: *Hi, Flash. Come in and have a cup of coffee.*

Far from resenting the use of his nickname, Flash is pleased. For all his swagger he feels ill at ease in this club, and 'Flash' carries with it the respect of his delinquent companions. The leader's use of it makes him feel at home, and also suggests that he will be accepted as he is. He would like some coffee, but feels that accepting it might imply more of an acceptance of the total situation than he is willing to give.

FLASH: *No, thanks. I just had some at the Spot.*

This is the name of the local café, and what Flash is pointing out is that he has his own base and does not need to come begging at the club. The club leader recognises this, but is not put off.

LEADER: *Well, have another. I'm just going to have one, and I'd like the company.*

This was a sound remark. By refusing to accept Flash's rebuff he showed that he was not easily put out. It was also a friendly remark. What is more, it established the relationship as one of mutual co-operation.

FLASH: *O.K. then . . . no sugar.*

As they walk to the canteen the leader points out some of the amenities. He does so in a carefully neutral way, neither implying that Flash should be grateful for the opportunities offered, nor begging him to join the club. He also tries to learn something of Flash's interests.

LEADER: *We've got quite a good record-player here and a whole stack of discs. What sort of music do you go for?*

(In Interview *A* the aunt would have said 'I suppose you like Elvis Presley.')

FLASH: *Oh, all sorts. I play the trumpet a bit myself.*

He is still pointing out that he has as much to offer the club himself as the club has to offer him.

> LEADER: *Do you know Shorty Page? He comes here quite a lot and he's quite good on the drums. You ought to get together one night.*

He has moved in a little too fast and Flash isn't buying it.

> FLASH (unenthusiastically): *Yeah . . . could be.*

This situation is best left alone, so the club leader changes the subject, making a mental note not to pressure Flash yet, but that this might be a good opening when the time comes. While they are sitting drinking their coffee, a very pretty girl comes in. Seeing Flash eyeing her, the leader thinks that she might also be an effective bait.

> LEADER: *That's Beryl. She's a real smart kid. She's very good on the piano too.*

This was a mistake. Flash is one of those youths who are secretly rather shy of and frightened by pretty girls, especially one as poised as Beryl. He thinks that as she can play the piano, his one social asset – being able to play the trumpet – might have lost its value, and so instead of being bait she becomes a major threat. The leader recognises that his remark has not gone down too well, but he does not know why. Knowing that it is touch and go whether Flash will ever be persuaded to come in off the streets, he plays the situation extremely carefully and spends the rest of the time available in maintaining a friendly and impersonal conversation.

Interview C

Twelve-year-old Frank has been referred to the school psychologist because he is working below his capacity. They are already well into the interview and the child has relaxed and is talking quite freely. The relationships at home appear good, and Frank spends his spare time in the usual pursuits of his age and culture.

PSYCHOLOGIST: *Let me see now, you have a younger
brother, David, haven't you? Isn't he in Grade
Three?*

FRANK: *Yes, he wants to be a chemist.*

There is a note of scorn in this remark, and the
psychologist picks it up.

PSYCHOLOGIST: *It sounds as if you don't think he'll
make it.*

FRANK: *You've got to be pretty good to be a chemist,
and he is only average.*

This sounds like sibling rivalry and could be highly
relevant, so the psychologist casts around to see what
will come up.

PSYCHOLOGIST: *Do you have any other brothers and
sisters?*

He knows the answer to this question, but he wants
to see what Frank will do with it.

FRANK: *Yes, there's Annette – she's married – and
then there's Geoffrey.*

Again there was a slight change in his expression
as he mentioned his older brother, and it is necessary
to find out why.

PSYCHOLOGIST: *What does Geoffrey do?*

FRANK: *He's a chemist.*

PSYCHOLOGIST: *Oh. Is that where David got the idea
from?*

FRANK: *Yes.*

PSYCHOLOGIST: *What do you want to do when you
leave school?*

FRANK: *Oh, I guess I'll work in a shop or something.*

The pattern is now beginning to fall into place. The
highly successful older brother is being held up at
home as a model that the younger boy should emulate,
and Frank feels so far inferior to him that he is giving
up in despair. Further questioning is needed to confirm

this impression and to find out whether the source of the comparison is Father or Mother or Geoffrey.

PSYCHOLOGIST: *What does your Dad want you to be?*

FRANK: *Oh, I don't know.*

PSYCHOLOGIST: *And your Mother, does she have any ideas?*

FRANK: *Oh, she doesn't mind.*

He answered the first question in a very off-hand manner and the second with some relief. It was evident that he was evading the first and covering up. It had already been established that the relationship between Frank and his father was good, so it would appear that there was friction only in this one area.

PSYCHOLOGIST: *Does your father put a lot of store by education, or does he think other things are just as important?*

This is a simple multiple-choice question that does not imply that Father *ought* to think one way or the other, so Frank is free to answer.

FRANK: *I guess he sets a lot of store by education.*

PSYCHOLOGIST: *What do you feel about it?*

FRANK: *Oh, yes, they're always telling you in the papers about school drop-outs not being able to get work and all that.*

By now it is evident that Frank would like to do better in school, and the psychologist risks summing up what the boy has been hinting at, but not quite saying.

PSYCHOLOGIST: *When you've got an older brother who's done well, it's pretty tough to come along afterwards, isn't it?*

FRANK (who has been sitting very still and tense during the previous few remarks, suddenly relaxes and grins): *It sure is.*

The feeling he puts into these few words and the

sudden relaxation of his body both confirm the tentative
diagnosis of the situation.

Interview D

A juvenile court judge is questioning a boy accused of
shop-breaking. The police evidence has been heard,
and the parents have said that they have done everything they can for the lad and are unable to control
him.

> JUDGE: *Well, you've heard what your father has to
> say. Aren't you ashamed of yourself?*
> BOY: *Yes.*
> JUDGE: *So you ought to be. Your parents have done
> everything they can, and this is how you repay
> them. Do you think that's right?*
> BOY: *No*
> JUDGE: *Well, what are you going to do about it?*
> (Boy does not answer.)
> *There's no use standing there. The world doesn't
> owe you a living, you know. You have to work hard
> to get on in this world. Why did you break into the
> shop anyway?*
> BOY: *I don't know.*

The judge has gone about things the wrong way
round. If he had asked his last question first, he might
have got some sort of answer. As it is, the boy knows
that he has not been given a chance to give his side of
the story before being bawled out by the judge. He is
convinced that anything he says will simply let loose
another tirade, so he keeps quiet.

> JUDGE: *You must know why you did it.*

The boy does not answer. Getting nowhere with
open questions, the judge tries some closed ones.

> JUDGE: *Did you want money? Don't you get a big
> enough allowance – is that it?*

His voice has now softened and the boy thinks that
perhaps he is trying to find out what went on after all.

JUDGE: *Whose idea was it? Was it yours?*
BOY: *No.*
JUDGE: *Was there somebody else with you?*
BOY: *Yes.*
JUDGE: *Who?*

The boy does not answer and the judge questions the police again. It appears that a neighbour thought he saw two boys, but could not be sure.

JUDGE: *Was this other boy older than you or younger?*
BOY: *Older.*
JUDGE: *How old was he?*
BOY: *Twenty.*
JUDGE: *Oh, that puts a very different light on the matter. What was his name?*

In spite of repeated probing the boy still refuses to answer. He is being prevented from doing so by a sense of loyalty to the young man concerned. He was not very anxious to take part in this offence anyway and regretted doing so as soon as he had begun; he went through it for fear of being called chicken. If the police officers who first questioned him or his parents or the judge had approached him with sympathy and understanding, he would almost certainly have broken down and given all the details. As it was, their hostility seemed to put him permanently in the enemy camp, and he now feels closer to the twenty-year-old than he does to anybody else. The judge might have been successful if he had started with a fact-finding interview and kept his caustic remarks until the boy had broken down; then they would have been far more effective.

Interview E

A police officer is interviewing a six-year-old who has apparently been sexually molested by a neighbour.

OFFICER: *What did he do?*

The little girl does not reply. She is obviously much too embarrassed.

OFFICER: *Did he touch you?*

She nods.

OFFICER: *Where? Show me.*

She points to her breasts and her legs.

OFFICER: *Did he touch you anywhere else?*

She shakes her head.

OFFICER: *Are you sure?*

She nods.

So far the interview has been conducted well. He has recognised that she finds it very hard to say anything, but he has not asked her any leading questions.

OFFICER: *Did he give you anything?*

MARY: *No.*

OFFICER: *Nothing at all?*

All he is doing is making sure of her answer, but she takes this as a criticism of the neighbour of whom she is really quite fond in spite of everything that has happened. So to defend him she says (untruthfully): *Yes, he gave me some candy.*

OFFICER: *Oh, he gave you some candy did he? Was it a lot of candy?*

MARY (still trying to put the neighbour in a good light): *Yes, a lot.*

Now the truth of the story is that Mary heard some of the other girls at school talking about sexual advances made by a man, and when this neighbour began a perfectly innocent rough-and-tumble game with her, she jumped to the conclusion that he too was making advances and told her mother, who went to the police. When the neighbour subsequently insisted that he was merely tickling her innocently and that she had never objected before, he was not believed because of the story about the candy. Looking

back over that section of the interview, it is hard to
see a major mistake that the police officer made.

However, he was wrong to carry out the interview
with the assumption that the man was guilty. When
the girl denied that the neighbour had 'touched her
anywhere else', the police officer probed with a further
question. But when she said that he gave her candy,
he accepted the answer immediately. 'Did he give
you anything?' was not strictly a leading question, but
with a six-year-old child, and in these circumstances,
it becomes one.

Interview F

A TV interviewer has an eight-year-old boy on his
show.

> INTERVIEWER: *Well; come along, Johnny, stand up
> here where the people can all see you.*
> BOY: *My name's Jimmy.*
> INTERVIEWER: *That's fine . . . that's fine, Johnny.
> Do you have any brothers and sisters?*

Jimmy was indignant when the man got his name
wrong the first time, but he is now furious. However,
he is too polite and well-mannered to say so and
answers politely.

> JIMMY: *Yes, one brother and one sister.*
> INTERVIEWER (winking at the camera): *I expect that
> you're cleverest of the lot aren't you?*
> JIMMY (trying to be fair): *I don't think so. Janey gets
> better marks than I do in school.*
> INTERVIEWER: *I'll bet you hate that. Do you pull her
> hair?* (Again he winks at the audience.)

If Jimmy's manners were as bad as the interviewer's,
he would turn around at this point and make equally
personal and insulting remarks about the relationship
between the interviewer and his wife. But unfortunately for the audience he does not do so. It is clear that the
interviewer has not heard a thing that Jimmy has said.

He has a series of ideas and questions and he throws
them at Jimmy because he thinks they will get a
laugh. He succeeds in this, and although the boy's
resentment may mean nothing to an entertainer it
would be disastrous in almost any other type of
interview.

Interview G

A Grade One teacher has heard that one of her pupils
has a drunken father and she takes the child aside
after school in the hope that she might be able to do
something about it.

TEACHER: *How are things going on at home?*

BRENDA (assuming that the teacher must be
asking about homework): *It was a bit hard last
week.*

TEACHER: *Is there anything I can do to help?*

Brenda is somewhat puzzled by this remark and
looks blank. After all, the teacher could set easier
homework if she wanted to.

TEACHER: *Does your Mommy get very upset?*

Brenda thinks this is a rather exaggerated way to
talk, but teachers are unpredictable beings anyway,
and it is true that Mother did tell her off a few weeks
ago for not finishing her arithmetic. She supposes that
this is what teacher is talking about.

BRENDA: *She does sometimes.*

TEACHER: *I wish you'd tell me about it.*

(Brenda does not reply.)

*I know your Daddy's sick — doctors can help
people like him.*

This confuses Brenda still further, because she
cannot imagine why her teacher has suddenly brought
Father into the picture, so she still says nothing.

TEACHER: *Does he hit you?*

Now her mother goes to great lengths to hide
Father's drinking from the neighbours, and Brenda

accepts this necessity. She resents the question, feeling it is none of her teacher's business.

BRENDA: *Oh, no!*

Her hostility is evident and the teacher is nonplussed by it because she thought she had been getting on so well before. She does not recognise, of course, that they were talking at cross-purposes.

Appendix A # An Interviewing Room

Many interviewers will have to use an office or another
room that was not designed for work with children.
This is unfortunate, because the wrong surroundings
limit the scope of techniques that can be used. A social
agency needs a room that can be used for children
presenting a variety of disorders, but is unlikely to
require facilities for the extremely disturbed child.
A child-guidance clinic, however, will include in its
case-load patients who are completely beyond control;
they may be suicidal, dangerous, or show a great range
of unusual behaviour. This appendix offers suggestions
to cover all these possibilities. The structural arrange-
ments are dealt with first, then the specialised equipment, and finally the furniture.[1]

For highly aggressive and destructive children it is
necessary to have everything breakable removed and
everything throwable tied down. However, these
precautions applied ostentatiously say to the child:
'I don't trust you an inch, and I have all my defences
prepared.' An aggressive child will immediately
respond by trying to find a chink in these defences.
These children are liable to break the windows, but
it is not necessary to have screens on the inside. Either
the windows can be made of armoured glass or else
they can be made of clear plastic that can be pushed

[1] Many of the recommendations are from W. C. M. Scott,
Canadian Psychiatric Association Journal VI 5 (1961),
pp. 281–6.

out and replaced with a minimum of difficulty. As there is always a danger that a child will jump out of the window or control the situation by threatening to, it is necessary to have an outside screen. This, however, can be made to appear identical with a fly-screen and will therefore not be provocative. There is some advantage in blocking the windows so that they cannot be opened more than a few inches, but this is a considerable disadvantage to people who have to work in the office.

Children will often avoid unpleasant interviews by the favourite device of going to the toilet. This is a hard request to refuse; not only on humanitarian grounds, but because the child can always smile sweetly afterwards and say, 'I told you so.' For this reason it is useful to have a toilet immediately accessible from the interviewing room.

Younger children like playing with water, and for them it is essential that the room contain a sink with one tap; to prevent an excessive flow of water there should be a separate control either outside the room or provided with a key so that only a moderate stream of tepid water will be available. The sink should be provided with a draining-board.

The light should be flush or fairly flush with the ceiling and either made of armoured glass or protected by an unobtrusive grill. Even if the children to be seen are reasonably normal and well behaved, there is some advantage in this precaution because one may want to play a riotous game at some point, and it is a pity to have to watch out for the light fixtures all the time.

The same consideration applies to heating. Children can stuff things down air vents or behind radiators or can fall over and bang their heads on them. The heating method will probably be determined by considerations outside the control of the interviewer,

but radiators should be enclosed; heat vents should
be protected by a grill and radiant-type heating should
be high up out of the child's reach.

The floor should be covered by non-absorbent
material, and the edge should be carefully water-
proofed.

A child can invent many games with sand and toy
people, and for this purpose one of the most versatile
pieces of equipment is a sand-tray .This should be
about 2′ 6″ square and 3″ deep. It should stand on
legs 2′ off the floor; it should be lined with metal so
that it is possible to mix water with the sand; it should
have a lid that can cover it completely and which can
be locked. This serves the double purpose of turning
the sand-tray into a useful table, and also of stopping
unruly children from throwing sand about.

Locked cupboards that will contain almost everything movable in the room should be provided. This
will allow the interviewer to have a great deal of
flexibility in the sort of atmosphere he creates,
because he can take toys out or put them away as the
situation demands. For example, if he has a small
occasional table he can put a teddy bear on it for a
small boy, a couple of dolls for a small girl, a few
miniature cars for an eight-year-old boy, or a copy of
Vogue or an ashtray for a teenager.

If children are to be seen for a number of interviews
(as they are in treatment) and if this involves any form
of play therapy, it is important that each child should
have his own drawer. These should be made about
2′ 6″ × 1′ 6″ × 9″. It is of some advantage if they are
completely removable and strong enough to be stood
upon. Between the drawers should be shelves, so it is
impossible to get to the drawer below them when the
drawer above is removed. Each drawer should be
locked, but can be provided with the same key. This

system will allow a child who has made a plasticine model or is in the middle of a painting, etc., to have it untouched, and even unseen, by any other child until he comes for the next interview.

Special problems require special additional facilities. It is sometimes useful to allow a fire-setter to set fires under carefully controlled circumstances. This will require a grate or other fireplace. There are other advantages in the fireplace. Not only does a fire make a room look much more cosy and welcoming, but nearly all children like playing with matches, and it is better to do so in the grate than on the desk. Children with fears of the dark can best be helped if the room can be completely blacked out. This requires a blackout screen for the window and the possibility of dimming the main light rather than simply switching it on and off.

Soundproofing the room is a great advantage. If one is interviewing a really noisy or exuberant child, it is annoying and frustrating to have to keep quietening him down because of one's colleagues in the next office.

A large blackboard, low enough for young children to reach easily, is essential. A notice-board on which important drawings can be displayed will save the conflict of upsetting the child by not putting them up or upsetting the administration by using thumb tacks in the plaster.

Most of these objects can be hidden fairly successfully. The sink can be in a cupboard and the blackboard and noticeboard can be hidden by drapes. These drapes or the drapes at the windows prove a temptation for many children; some will try to pull them down, others will try to climb up them. The best way of avoiding difficulties is to have them fixed onto the runners by large press-studs, so that if the child pulls on them they will simply come 'unpopped' and can be replaced easily. They should, of course, be easily washable.

It should go without saying (but in fact it needs to be said) that doctors should not have any of the more ghastly instruments lying within full sight or sticking casually out of their pockets.

A large doll's house is of great value. It is far better to make one's own out of 5-ply; the walls should be fitted into grooves so that rooms of different shapes and sizes can be set up at will. The furniture inside should be sturdy and simple; it will have to be tossed about, bombed, stood upon, and bitten. It should be possible to dismantle the whole house easily so that it can be put away in a small space when not needed.

A collapsible 'Wendy' house with room inside for the interviewer and child is of use if the interviewer is sufficiently flexible to spend most of his interviewing day in a foetal position.

The doll family should be as unbreakable as possible and supplied with removable clothes. They should, of course, fit the furniture. Nothing is more frustrating than a doll that is the wrong size or that cannot be bent into a sitting or other useful position. (It is an odd thing that although therapists are so ostentatiously matter-of-fact about sex, nudity, and so on, and expect the children to talk freely about them, we provide them with dolls without genitalia; this is an example of non-verbal communication to the effect that it would be much better if such things did not exist, contradicting our verbal protestations.) The doll family should include mother, father, brothers, sisters, babies, grandparents, aunts, uncles, and so on; an extra father or mother comes in useful if it reflects the child's own experiences. It is possible to make doll families from pipe-cleaners, wrapping them with

H

cotton wool and securing them with adhesive tape.

It is possible to draw up a long list of the toys that can be used during an interview. Nothing, however, can substitute for imagination and creativity on the part of the interviewer. The most versatile material is plasticine. This can be turned into people, animals, buildings, guns, ships, cars, trees, knives, food – anything in fact that might conceivably be needed. The people can be made any size, put into any position, chopped in half and reconstituted. Objectionable ones can be squashed flat on the desk with a very satisfying feeling. Plasticine is waterproof and insoluble and can be used in conjunction with water play. Its only disadvantage is that, once mixed with sand, it cannot be cleaned, but I, personally, think it has so many advantages that I use it in preference to the sand-tray.

In psychologists' language this material is 'unstructured'. Building bricks are also unstructured in a sense because they can be turned into any sort of building. If the room is big enough (or if a large enough storage cupboard is available near by), it is useful to have several large hollow cubes with holes in the sides, so that they can be lifted easily. They should be made of 5-ply or some other strong material; the sharp edges should be sanded down, and it is important to use a wood that does not splinter. With the addition of a few short planks the child and the interviewer can build ships, forts, houses, etc.

For less active children, scissors, a good supply of paper, water paints, and crayons are essential. A toy telephone intrigues some children, and it is not unusual for them to be able to talk to the interviewer 'through' the telephone and say things they cannot bring themselves to say directly to his face.

For older children and teenagers, one needs objects that the housekeeping magazines call 'conversation

pieces'. It matters little what these are because their
use is simply to enable the interviewer to start, if he
wishes, on an informal conversational note. One
therapist advocated the use of a dog and wrote a paper
entitled 'The Dog as Co-therapist'. This was greeted
with considerable derision, but in fact I too have found
animals to be most useful and versatile pieces of
equipment. The dog must be chosen for his personality
rather than for his pedigree; nothing could be more
welcoming to a child than a dog who wags his tail
when a child walks in. A cat is better than nothing,
although cats tend to be unresponsive and rejecting
animals, and are more liable to retaliate without
warning if a clumsy or hostile child hurts them. Even
a goldfish in a bowl has its points. It does not have to
be house-trained and keeps quiet. On the other hand it
is all too easily upset (the bowl, not the goldfish). It
must be remembered that some children are irrationally afraid of animals and will be upset even by a
family dog who is practically immobilised by old age.
For these reasons it is important to ask the child first
if he likes dogs (or whatever else it might be) before
you introduce them to each other. Apart from their
value as conversation pieces, pets often provide a
setting in which the child demonstrates how he gives
and receives affection.

Some people like a supply of games such as chess,
checkers, ludo, and so on. In my opinion these are
much more trouble than they are worth. It is very
easy for a child to avoid any sort of contact with the
interviewer by playing these games session after
session, and they are much too impersonal to give
any more information than the child's attitude to
competition, winning, or losing. Once in a while a
child will chatter on while playing these games but
become tongue-tied if given nothing else to do but

talk. However, the same advantage can be found in any other material that does not have the disadvantages just mentioned.

The furniture, generally, should be comfortable, easily cleaned, and as indestructible as possible. Heavy old armchairs are much better than light modern seats. It is possible to curl up in them, and impossible to throw them around. Leather is tough and easily cleaned. Generally speaking, modern plastics are not so tough and always tend to feel a bit chilly; loose covers can be substituted. In this case, beware of pins!

An old wooden desk is probably better than a metal one. In either case the drawers must be lockable. Wood is more easily chipped, cut, and stained than metal, but if there are enough chips, cuts, and stains to begin with a few more will not seem out of place. In my opinion, a metal desk tends to give a rather cold and clinical impression.

The final consideration has to be given to the interviewer's clothes. There is no point in having the room and its furniture proof against paint, water, sand, and violence, if the interviewer is wearing his best suit. As with the room itself, his clothes should not be ostentatiously defensive. Difficulty arises because he may be interviewing, during the day, several people who are going to approach him very differently. Gardening clothes suitable for work with a paint-throwing child may offend a member of the Board. If you are going to crawl around the floor it is necessary to wear clothes that can be crawled around in. Anybody who thinks he can interview children and maintain his dignity had better find a different job.

On the other hand it is equally inappropriate to interview (for example) a smart and clothes-conscious teen-aged girl when one is wearing a paint-spattered shirt and dust-covered trousers. It is often overlooked

that one can be perfectly clean and respectable without
dressing as if one were working in a bank or a fashion
salon. For men, an open-neck shirt and slacks are more
versatile than collar, tie, and suit. (It is hard to keep
one's hold on life, let alone one's dignity, if a child
grabs your tie and pulls.) Parents and administrators
are liable to have such a rigid idea of a 'responsible'
doctor or psychologist that they are shocked by such
frivolity. However, you can't please everybody all the
time. My own practice is to wear something serviceable
and comfortable of this sort, and to wear a long lab
coat in addition if I am going to become intimately
involved with paint, water, and mud.

Observing Children

When untrained staff are asked to prepare a report on a child's behaviour or to record an interview, they often ask, 'What should I put down?' This list of points is comprehensive; it includes not only observations that might be made in an office interview, but also those that can be made when children are playing in a group. Finally, for completeness, it includes observations that could be made only in a residential setting.

Notice and record the positive as well as the negative aspects of his behaviour. That is to say, do not be concerned only with abnormalities.

In reporting or in comparing notes with other staff, be clear that you are using the same definitions for the words you employ.

Do not confuse observation with the inferences you draw. For example, it is a factual observation to say, 'Johnny hit another boy.' It is an inference to say, 'Johnny was angry.' The inference may or may not be the correct one.

The following list[1] of things to watch for will seem overwhelming and impossible to the inexperienced observer. It is impossible to remember, even if one notices, a series of unrelated facts. As you become more familiar with different types of behaviour or pathological syndromes, it will be easier to remember

[1] Modified from Nancy Trevorrow Carbonara, *Techniques for Observing Normal Child Behaviour* (University of Pittsburgh Press, 1961).

them in groups like this. It is important, of course, not
to 'fill in the gaps' by recording observations that
ought to be there because you have already reached
a conclusion about the condition the child is showing.
It is helpful for two or more inexperienced observers
to watch the same group of children for the same
period and to compare notes afterwards to see what
they each noticed.

Appearance

Note the child's dress. Does he seem to be in good
physical health? If not, in what way is he abnormal?
What are his facial expressions? Note his characteristic
and usual expression and also the changes that occur
in certain circumstances. Is he alert, placid, vacant,
attentive, sulky, anxious, or suspicious? If his expression changes, what circumstances bring this about?
Does he have any special grimaces or tics?

Movement

Is he quick or slow? Is he well co-ordinated? Is he
restless? (Remember that it is just as important to
record that a child has particularly good co-ordination,
e.g. in throwing or catching a ball, as it is to notice
poor co-ordination.) Does he show any repetitive
movements, such as scratching or rubbing? Does he
have any mannerisms with his hands? Do his movements and attitudes have an obvious purpose or
meaning? Does he move freely, or is he inhibited?

Relationships

How does he respond to other children? Does he seek
out individuals or mix with the group? Is he the leader,
does he boss them around, or is he a follower? Does
he withdraw from the group, or is he rejected by
them? Does he choose a particular sort of child or a
child of a different age from himself for a friend? Does
he prefer boys to girls, or the other way around?

How does he get on with the staff? Is he friendly or

fearful; is he clinging or is he a teacher's pet? How does he respond to rules and to limits? Is he over-concerned about them, accept them reasonably, or does he show a passive resistance? Is he subversive or openly rebellious?

Activities

How does he accept the programme? Does he just 'go along' with it or does he join in enthusiastically? Does he try to break it up? Does he show initiative and suggest new ideas? Which particular games, lessons, and activities produce which type of response? How does he respond to frustration? Can he accept it, and if not, what does he do about it? What particular sorts of frustration seem to be upsetting for him (e.g. losing a game)? What sort of play activities does he prefer? Has he any special skills? Does he concentrate well? Does he actually avoid certain activities, and if so, which ones? What does he seem to get out of them (e.g. is it competition, a mastery of the techniques, or does he like them because he can let off steam)? Does he gain any particular sensory pleasure from them, such as he might from handling clay? Does he show particular creativity? If so, in what media? Is he distractable; does he try to do more than one thing at a time? In his games or other activities does he seem to be preoccupied with one particular situation or role? For example, is he always playing the part of a baby, a tiger, a clown, or a wicked father? Do his drawings have a recurrent theme, such as people being murdered? (Interpretation of drawings and other creative activities is extremely difficult and compli-cated. Nevertheless, it is well worth studying them carefully to see what can be noted.)

Talk

Record the form of what he says, as well as the content. For example, does he say a lot or a little? Does he talk

spontaneously, and if so, to whom; or does he wait to
be asked questions? Is his conversation coherent or
confused? Does he fall into sudden silences, or keep
changing the subject? What does his conversation
indicate about his particular interests or fears? What
conclusions can you reach about his intelligence,
maturity, and cultural background from his conversation?

Mood

What appears to be his characteristic mood? Is there
any inconsistency between his appearance and how
he describes it? For example, he may appear frightened,
but strongly deny it. Is his mood fairly constant,
or does it fluctuate, and if so, what makes it do so?
Does he show a greater emotional response than
one would expect in a child of his age in the particular
circumstances?

**Special
symptoms**

Does he show any evidence of delusions, hallucina-
tions, or compulsions? Does he frequently misinterpret the environment? For example, if another child
bumps into him by accident, does he take this as delib-
erate?

Orientation

Does he show any confusion about where he is,
how to get from one place to another, or the time of
day?

Eating

Is his appetite good, poor, or excessive? Is he faddy?
Are there particular foods that he likes or dislikes?
Does he use the mealtime as a special occasion on
which to be difficult or to show special relationships
with staff or other children?

Sleeping

Does he sleep soundly or restlessly? Does he have
nightmares? Is he afraid of the dark? Does he show

special types of behaviour at bedtime? For example, he may accept 'mothering' then, whereas he will not accept it at other times of the day. Are there any particular symptoms associated with sleeping (e.g. talking in his sleep or grinding his teeth)? Does he wet the bed?

Books on the Subject

The more one knows about children the more
effectively one can interview them, but even somebody
specialising in this field cannot hope to know everything. The non-specialist should, however, have a
working knowledge of child development; in my view
the best single book on this subject is *Child Development and Personality* by Mussen and Conger, which
presents a good balance between psychoanalytic
theories and experimental approaches. It also contains
a very large number of references that will enable the
reader to carry his studies further.

There are many excellent books on psychiatric
techniques that are used with children, but they will
not be listed here because they are too esoteric for the
non-specialist, and the specialist will have his own
references to them. There is one, however, that is
worth noting because it is about adolescents; most of
the child psychiatry textbooks give little or no
guidance on work with this age-group. This is Holmes'
The Adolescent in Psychotherapy. Although it is
written for the psychiatrist, its common-sense
approach and obvious basis of experience would be of
great value to anybody working with adolescents,
even if he has no intention of undertaking therapy.
Another specialist book that can be read with profit by
the non-specialist is Redl's *When We Deal with
Children*. This is a recent collection of articles and
other work that have been previously published.

Much of it is not particularly relevant to interviewing,
but it is worth reading because of Redl's valuable
emphasis on the fact that many children and teenagers
cannot be successfully confined to the office – he calls
his techniques 'Life-Space Interviewing'.

Books on interviewing almost always assume that the
subject is an adult, but many of the rules and suggestions apply to children. There has been a great change
in them in the last thirty years; for example, Young
writing in 1935 could say, 'No scientific studies of the
best methods of analysing interviews or interviewing
have as yet been made.' This is no longer true. Her
book, *Interviewing in Social Work*, is comprehensive
and readable, but in the light of recent work seems
somewhat woolly. A similar book is by Fenlason,
Essentials in Interviewing, which was based on an
undergraduate course at the University of Minnesota.
The style is somewhat stuffy, but it is relieved by
frequent quotations from a wide range of sources. At
the other extreme are such books as *The Focussed
Interview*, by Merton and others. This work originally
arose from communications research and propaganda
analysis, but it has been rewritten. Its approach is
essentially analytic and scientific; the authors are
concerned to discover which stimulus or pattern of
stimuli in the total situation lead to observable effects.
A book like this sharpens our perceptions and scientific
understanding, but the overall effect is somewhat cold
and impersonal; at the opposite extreme are two books
by Elizabeth and Karl de Schweinitz, *Interviewing in
Social Security* and a shorter adaptation of this, *Interviewing in the Social Services*. These are both excellent
in that they show a warm and very human attitude
to the client that must have been of enormous help to
the social service field-workers for whom they were
written. Unfortunately they are both much too short

to have room for detailed discussion. Both of them
have become classics in the field; others are Rogers'
Counselling and Psychotherapy and Rice's much older
book, *Methods in Social Science.*

There are also books dealing with specialised types
of interviews; one example is that by Adams, *Interviewing Procedures,* which is concerned with survey
interviewing, but does have a good description of the
rationale behind the technique and is therefore worth
looking at. Harms and Schreiber recently put out
Handbook of Counselling Techniques, which consists
of thirty-six essays dealing with different situations,
such as marriage guidance, interviewing from the
points of view of different religions, and so on. Seven
of these essays deal with children. Unfortunately
these seven are very disappointing; for example the
essay by Richard R. Korn on interviewing juvenile
delinquents is really a brief and superficial account of
juvenile delinquency, with very little emphasis on the
actual techniques of interviewing in this field. The
other essays include suggestions on giving advice to
parents about bringing up their children, counselling
in schools and camps, in colleges, and in child-protec-
tion services.

One of the best books on general interviewing is by
Kahn and Cannell, *The Dynamics of Interviewing.*
It is readable, clear, and pointed and has a good
bibliography, including reference to recent experimental work. It also conceives of interviewing in a
broad sense (unlike most of the books written by and
for social workers or psychiatrists) and by way of
examples gives a detailed account of a medical interview, two personnel interviews (one with an experienced and the other with an inexperienced
applicant), a supervisor-subordinate interview, and a
social work interview.

Apart from the books that are directly related to interviewing children, there is no end to the books that may be read with profit. An enormous amount is already known about the way children think. Jean Piaget's work alone covers many volumes. The behaviour therapists are pouring out a torrent of papers and books dealing with the sorts of situations and stimuli that make children behave in one way or another. There are books on children's play, on their lore and language, on different types of parent-child relationship and the consequences, on the ways in which children behave in different types of educational milieu; books that help us to understand delinquents, novels that help us see the world through the eyes of one particular adolescent, and so on and so on.

Bibliography

ADAMS, J. Stacy, *Interviewing Procedures*. University of North Carolina Press, Chapel Hill, 1958.

DE SCHWEINITZ, Elizabeth and Karl, *Interviewing in Social Security*. U.S. Department of Health, Education and Welfare, Washington, D.C., 1961.

DE SCHWEINITZ, Elizabeth and Karl, *Interviewing in the Social Services*. National Council of Social Service, London, 1962.

FENLASON, Anne F., *Essentials in Interviewing*. Harper, New York, 1952.

GARRETT, Annette, *Interviewing: Its Principles and Methods*. Family Service Association of America, New York, 1962.

HARMS, Ernest, and SCHREIBER, P., *Handbook of Counselling Techniques*. Macmillan Co., New York, 1963.

HOLMES, Donald J., *The Adolescent in Psychotherapy*. Little Brown, Boston, 1964.

KAHN, Robert L., and CANNELL, C. F., *The Dynamics of Interviewing*. Wiley, New York and London, 1961.

119 Books on the Subject

MERTON, Robert K., FISKE, M., and KENDALL, P. L., *The Focussed Interview*. Free Press, Glencoe, Ill., 1956.

Methods in Social Science, ed. S. A. Rice. University of Chicago Press, Chicago, 1931.

MUSSEN, Paul Henry, and CONGER, J. Janeway, *Child Development and Personality*. Harper, New York, 1956.

REDL, Fritz, *When We Deal with Children*. Free Press, New York and Collier-Macmillan, London, 1966.

ROGERS, Carl R., *Counselling and Psychotherapy*. Houghton Mifflin Co., Boston, 1942.

YOUNG, Pauline V., *Interviewing in Social Work*. McGraw-Hill, New York and London, 1935.

Index

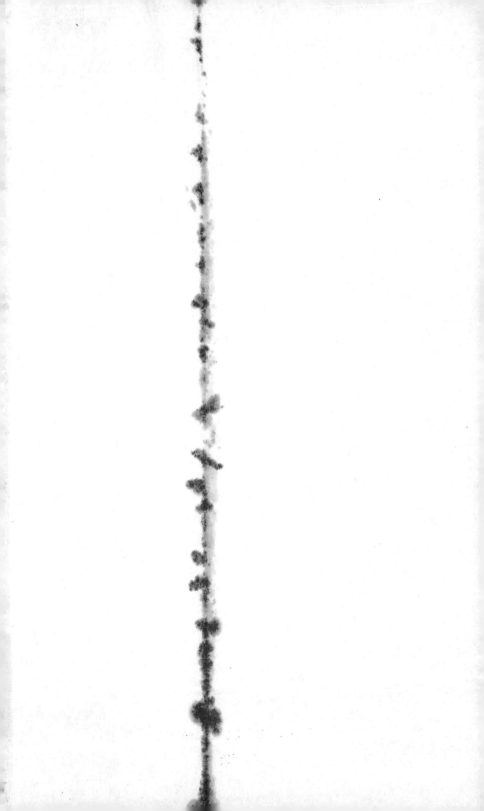

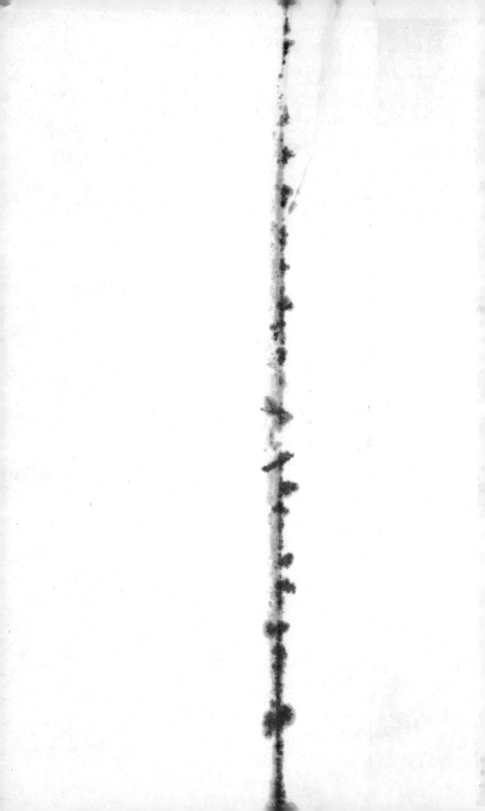